PROCLAMATION COMMENTARIES

- The New Testament
Witnesses for Preaching   Gerhard Krodel, *Editor*

MARK

Paul J. Achtemeier

FORTRESS PRESS   Philadelphia, Pennsylvania

To my son,
who bears that
goodly name

COPYRIGHT © 1975 BY FORTRESS PRESS

Library of Congress Catalog Card Number 74-26333

ISBN 0-8006-0581-0

Second printing 1976

5893E76   Printed in U.S.A.   1-581

CONTENTS

	Editor's Foreword	v
1.	Some Preliminary Reflections	1
2.	The Intention of Mark's Gospel	11
3.	Mark's Method of Creating a Narrative	22
4.	The Structure of Mark	31
5.	The Christology of Mark	41
6.	Jesus as Preacher	51
7.	Jesus as Teacher	60
8.	Jesus as Miracle Worker	71
9.	The Passion of Jesus	82
10.	The Disciples in Mark	92
11.	The Parousia in Mark	101
12.	Some Literary Problems	111
	Selected Bibliography	118
	Index	120

EDITOR'S FOREWORD

The insights of contemporary New Testament scholarship are stored in learned journals such as the *Journal of Biblical Literature, Seminar Papers of the Society of Biblical Literature, New Testament Studies, Novum Testamentum, Zeitschrift für Neutestamentliche Wissenschaft und die Kunde des Urchristentums,* and many others. For the parish pastor who week after week is challenged to proclaim the message of a particular text, the concerns and insights of present day New Testament scholarship are not readily available.

The series *Proclamation: Aids for Interpreting the Lessons of the Church Year,* published by Fortress Press, and similar endeavors are one way in which scholarship seeks to support the church's kerygmatic task. This new series of *Proclamation Commentaries* will serve as companion volumes to the *Proclamation: Aids.* Each commentary will deal with the witness of a particular book or section of the New Testament and the issues which contemporary scholarship has discerned in studying that material. These commentaries do not give verse by verse interpretations, but seek to draw the reader into the discussion of significant themes found in a particular segment of the New Testament literature and thus prepare him to understand the kind of exegesis which he will find in *Proclamation: Aids.* For this reason the first two chapters of this volume on Mark deal with methods and should be read with Mark's Gospel at hand.

Studies in Mark are at present undergoing a thorough reexamination of earlier conclusions and are probing not only after the intentions of the traditions which were used by the second evangelist, but also after his own intentions and purposes in assembling and modifying those traditions and producing the book which we know as the Gospel according to Mark. The present volume does not claim to contain the "assured results of scholarship" but is rather a progress

v

report to those engaged in the pastoral work of the church, giving an account of Mark's witness as seen by contemporary scholarship. Hence it contains questions which remain open because the present state of our knowledge of Mark does not warrant definitive conclusions.

The format of the book has prevented the author from acknowledging his debt to the fraternity of international and interdenominational scholars who have wrestled with the witness of Mark. The annotated bibliography gives at least a partial acknowledgment of those who have labored before and alongside the author in understanding that witness.

Paul J. Achtemeier is Professor of New Testament at Union Theological Seminary, Richmond, Virginia. He has been a member of the task force on the study of Mark's Gospel of the Society of Biblical Literature and is the author of significant articles on the witness of the Second Gospel.

GERHARD KRODEL
Lutheran Theological Seminary at Philadelphia

CHAPTER ONE

SOME PRELIMINARY REFLECTIONS

It is not self-evident that the kind of writing we designate with the term "gospel" should have been produced. From all we can gather, the earliest followers of the risen Christ expected this world to pass away, and God's kingdom, his rule, to be established visibly in place of contemporary political structures. Under those circumstances, writing a fully detailed sequential record to preserve an accurate memory of past events would not seem appropriate. When God's rule came, of which Jesus of Nazareth had been the final sign, who would really be interested in its foreshadowings, and in the period of time between Jesus' resurrection and his return in glory? Who would want to read of the first glimmerings of God's kingdom when they themselves were enjoying its full presence?

In such a situation, attention must have been focused on the future, rather than the past. The present was a time for preparation, and for telling others the good news so they, too, could prepare themselves. Such, for example, seems to have been the motivation of the apostle Paul who, convinced the end was coming soon, perhaps even during his lifetime, found in that fact the necessary motivation for a missionary activity of broadest scope. It is clear that Paul was not alone in such activity. Evidently such a missionary impulse was inherent in the earliest understanding of faith in Jesus, crucified and risen.

If, however, there was a lack of interest in the exact sequence of historical events, there was no lack of interest, particularly within the missionary thrust of the faith, in Jesus himself, whose return would inaugurate God's reign visibly on earth. The coming Lord was Jesus, who had already lived in Palestine, and thus a missionary call to accept the Christian interpretation of events would unavoidably involve some discussion of this Jesus, what he had said and what he had done. If he were the first ray of the dawning kingdom, one could gain some indication of the contours of that kingdom from what he was like. In that way, specific sayings or anecdotes about Jesus, which would aid in such missionary preaching, would very soon find wide circulation as Christian missionaries began to penetrate the Mediterranean world. Hints of the way such materials would be used can again be found in Paul. Sayings of the Lord would be applied in order to solve problems that arose within early Christian communities, as is the case in 1 Cor. 7:10 and 9:14. Traditions about Jesus' activities would be used as guidelines for the activities of groups that looked for his speedy return, as in 1 Cor. 11:23–25. Such traditions would also be used to provide guidelines for the contours of the faith itself, indicating what was essential to it, as in 1 Cor. 15:3–7.

In this way, a large body of material concerning things Jesus said and did, as well as traditions about what had happened to him, would be accumulated. That in itself is not very surprising. The Hellenistic world regularly collected such stories about religious as well as secular heroes; indeed such a distinction carried less force in that world than it does in ours. Sayings of rabbis and philosophers, deeds of men favored by the gods, and by God, were common in that world, and were used in efforts to promote and defend the framework of religious conviction to which they bore witness.

What is perhaps surprising is the freedom with which the sayings of Jesus were used, with little or no interest in the historical circumstances within which he said them, or within which some specific event happened. Paul again can show us how this was carried on. Paul in no way feels himself bound, when quoting a word of Jesus, to limit its application to the precise way in which Jesus used it. Paul does not even indicate he knew such particulars. When he quotes a word of Jesus about divorce, he applies it unquestioningly to the situation in Corinth, and to those who believe in the risen Christ. Nor did Paul feel himself bound to his knowledge of the sayings of Jesus when it came to dealing with problems arising within that community of believers. He was quite free to deal with problems about which he knew no saying or event in the life of Jesus to guide him, as in 1 Cor. 7:12, 25.

Clearly, Paul, and other missionaries like him, felt a certain freedom over against the traditions about Jesus, what he had said and done. We will also confront that freedom if we compare materials in

the three synoptic Gospels, Matthew, Mark, and Luke. Lack of antiquarian interest alone will not explain such freedom. By what right
did people ignore the context of the life of Jesus that had produced
this material, and even more, by what right did they change the form,
and when it seemed appropriate, that very context itself, in reporting
what Jesus had done and said? The answer lies in the very heart of
the Christian faith itself: the conviction that death was unable to hold
Jesus, and that God had raised and exalted Jesus to his own right
hand, whence Jesus would come to usher in God's rule. The central
affirmation of the faith, therefore, did not celebrate a dead hero, but a
living Lord. Christian missionary traditions did not collect around the
memory of a great man, now gone, of whom all we have are rem-
iniscences of what he said and did. Rather, those traditions were used
to announce that this same Jesus would very soon return, this Jesus
who now lived with God.

If Jesus were now alive, then he must continue to exercise guidance
over those who followed him. He must continue to teach his flock, as
he had taught them in the past. Indeed, only in the light of the
knowledge that he is the risen, ruling Lord could anything of his
earthly life be understood. While this is made explicit in only two of
the Gospels (Luke 24:13–27, esp. vv. 25–27, and vv. 44–45; John
14:25–26; 16:12–14; cf. 2:22), it seems nevertheless to underlie
the understanding of those who formulated and handed on the synoptic traditions as a whole. If the resurrection provided the keystone of
the Christian faith, giving meaning to all other traditions (cf. 1 Cor.
15:14, 17), then nothing of that tradition can be understood apart
from that event. Faith in Jesus risen and ruling thus colored the
presentation of materials recalled from his earthly career, but it also
gave to those who used such traditions the freedom to use and adapt
them to new situations. The risen Christ was present among those
who believed in him. He continued to teach and guide them as he had
before his crucifixion. He continued as the living Lord of his church,
guiding and directing it as he had his band of followers in Galilee. It
was this conviction that allowed those early Christians to reshape, as
need arose, the traditions about Jesus, in order to reflect his ongoing
guidance of their lives and their fate. Therefore, it was not ignorance
or carelessness that allowed the traditions about what Jesus did and
said to be reshaped to meet new conditions, but the burning convic-

tion that Jesus as risen Lord continued to speak to his church through the Holy Spirit present among believers. As Jesus had spoken before to his followers in Galilee, so as the risen Christ he continued to speak to them through the Spirit that inspired in them the appropriate words. We can see how this was understood in such a place as Mark 13:11, or Gal. 2:20.

The traditions about Jesus, therefore, remembered in the time of missionary activity, understood in the light of his resurrection, and used in the framework of a faith whose basic conviction centered on Jesus risen and exalted, were employed by the primitive church in the conviction that they could continue, with the guidance of the Spirit given to the church, to speak in Jesus' name the words needed by his followers. Adaptations of the traditions about Jesus hence were carried on, not carelessly or haphazardly, but in the conviction that that same Jesus could and did continue to speak to his followers. We will have frequent occasion in the following pages to follow some of those adaptations as the tradition moves from earlier to later stages in its transmission.

The remembering and transmitting of small individual units of tradition is one thing; combining them in the larger framework of a gospel is another. Something must have occurred which made it imperative to preserve such traditions within a larger interpretative framework. The actual act of writing is not the crucial point, as though up to that point the primitive church had managed to do without any written materials at all. Paul's letters, for example, probably antedate the earliest of our Gospels by anywhere from ten to twenty-five years. The need for further instruction in nascent Christian communities, when distances prohibited Paul from getting there himself, made the epistolary form quite natural. Letters soon appeared within the overall Christian community, and their usefulness in turn led to that form being adopted for theological treatises (e.g., Hebrews). The epistolary form in which these Pauline materials are couched is the familiar one of the Hellenistic world. With the epistle, therefore, the church simply took over a form already in existence, and used it to express its own particular concerns.

To be sure, that is not the case for the gospel as a literary form. Religious literature flooded the Hellenistic world. The Jewish matrix within which the Christian faith was born, however, and within which it spent its earliest years, offers nothing to compare with what we have in our NT as "Gospels." That is not to say there was no interest in the sayings of wise teachers; a tractate such as the *Pirke Aboth* ("Sayings of the Fathers") in the Mishnah (the codification, about AD 220, of rabbinic oral traditions about the law) shows the care with which such sayings were remembered and handed on. Similarly, there was great interest in the wondrous deeds of such men as Hanina ben Dosa or Honi the Circle-Maker, as the many incidents remembered of them and preserved in the Talmud (the collection, based on the divisions of the Mishnah, of a vast amount of Jewish religious and folk traditions) clearly show.

The Hellenistic world into which the Christian faith moved within the first decade or two of its life, while producing a variety of kinds of literature, religious and secular, offered a similar paucity of models for our canonical Gospels. A form of literature called the "novel" or "romance" was in its formative stages about this time, a form which bears some resemblance in type and structure to our Gospels, but it flowered as a form only after the canonical Gospels had already been written, and had much greater influence on the later, non-canonical acts of the various apostles, such as the Acts of Paul and Thecla, the Acts of Thomas, the Acts of Peter, and many others. From a literary point of view, our Gospels belong as much to the formative stage of this literary type as they do to a genre which was established before the Gospels were written.

There was, in short, no set kind of literary form to which the author of the first Gospel could turn, as did Paul and others when they made use of the form of the epistle. Furthermore, as the Pauline letters show, at that point in the development of the church the individual stories and sayings about Jesus, floating without any kind of context, met the needs, theological and missionary, of that time. There is no indication in Paul that anything more about Jesus was needed. Why, then, a gospel?

While we cannot, at this point, do more than give a general answer to that question, there are some hints as to why a gospel like Mark's would become appropriate, and even necessary, as the early church grew and matured in its theological reflections about Jesus of Nazareth, risen and reigning. A growing church, for example, would need to cover, with its authoritative materials about Jesus, a wider geographical range than the custodians of such memories, the apostles and their immediate followers, could responsibly cover. Again, as new converts began to proclaim their faith, some check would be needed on the accuracy with which they presented the material about Jesus of Nazareth. The disappearance through death of those who had known Jesus, and who served as the wellspring and check on the traditions about him, may also have served to add impetus to the desire to have some organized presentation of the traditions about him. The Pauline letters, and the earlier traditional materials they contain (e.g., Phil. 2:6–11, a pre-Pauline hymn or confession of faith) emphasize Jesus as preexistent, and as risen and regnant, with almost no reference to the deeds and words of Jesus' earthly career. A desire, awakened by hearing Jesus thus proclaimed, to know more about him during his period as man in Palestine may also have contributed to the final creation of the literary form we know as "gospel."

All of these and more may have influenced the production of the Gospel according to Mark. Some historical crisis also could have precipitated its writing. Such a crisis could have been internal or external; both existed within the time of the primitive church. We know of an internal crisis that occupied the church for some time and was fraught with the gravest consequences for the kind of church the young community was to become: the crisis of the place of Judaism within Christianity. Did one have to become a Jew first, in order to be a Christian? This concerned Paul deeply, as it concerned the early church, and its resolution was reached with the utmost seriousness and gravity (Galatians 2; Acts 15). A similar internal crisis, unrecorded in the few documents we possess about the beginnings of the church, could have precipitated a "gospel" as the only way to preserve correct faith, or open a necessary new stage in the life of the faithful community. An external crisis, such as the fall of Jerusalem, could also have had sufficient force within the primitive church to force it to cope with the new situation by means of a new form of literature. Any one of the many minor crises that led up to the outbreak of rebellion in AD 66 in Palestine might also have had sufficient impact on the community of which the author of Mark was a member, so that the only solution was the presentation of the traditions about Jesus in a totally new way.

Whatever the crisis may have been, the result was something new within the Christian community: a collection of the words and deeds of Jesus, along with some traditions about things that happened to him (e.g., baptism, transfiguration, crucifixion), arranged in a rough chronological sequence. For the first time that we can determine, the Jesus traditions were understood as a "story" in the Gospel of Mark, thus imprinting upon the faith a self-understanding that was to have profound and lasting consequences.

As we have already implied, the first of these "gospels" appears to be the one we know as "Mark." While scholars are not in total agreement that this is the case (some few want to insist on the priority of Matthew), most responsible NT scholars would agree that the evidence gathered by a comparison of the synoptic Gospels is best interpreted if Mark is assumed to be one of the sources used by Luke and Matthew. Such Markan priority cannot be finally and definitively "proved" on the basis of the materials we now possess, but that assumption has proved to be most likely, and continues to be most fruitful as a working hypothesis. A review of the relevant data in any good introduction to the NT (such as Kümmel; second edition recently published by Abingdon) will show what evidence there is, and what the various suggestions are about how it ought to be interpreted.

There is more importance to that conclusion than simply the solution of a literary and historical riddle, however. If Mark is the first Gospel, then he wrote with no knowledge of the form the traditions were to take in either Matthew or Luke, both written perhaps some twenty or thirty years later. That means that if we are to have any hope of recovering the points Mark wanted to make when he organized the Jesus traditions in this way for the first time, we will have to read Mark all by itself, with no reference to the way that material is presented in either Matthew or Luke. One useful way of understanding both Matthew and Luke is to see them primarily as commentaries on Mark, seeking to interpret his message for other readers by re-presenting the Markan materials, and by including other, further traditions about Jesus. Each of them has its own reason for reinterpreting the Markan traditions, however, and that reason will be different from the reason that caused Mark to shape the traditions as he has, or there would have been no need for a new edition of the "gospel." Thus, a comparison of similar materials in all three Gospels will help to throw light on the new emphases Matthew and Luke sought to give to the Jesus traditions, and in some cases, by seeing those new emphases, we may be helped to see the original Markan emphasis more clearly. But we must also, if we are to understand *Mark*, take care not to interpret him, or understand him, in the light of the reinterpretation his material underwent at the hands of Luke and Matthew. We cannot, therefore, if we are to understand Mark's intention, read him in the light of the way Matthew or Luke understood him, or seek to fill out "gaps" in the Markan presentation by using materials found in the other two Gospels. That way of proceeding can only confuse an attempt to see what Mark was trying to say, and is totally insufficient as a device for recovering the underlying "history," as will become clear in succeeding chapters.

Perhaps an example will help clarify and illustrate this point. All three synoptic Gospels contain the account of Jesus and his disciples going through a grainfield on the sabbath (Mark 2:23–28; Matt. 12:1–8; Luke 6:1–5). While it is clear in Matthew that the reason for the disciples' plucking the grain was their hunger (12:1b), and just as clear in Luke that they ate the grain they plucked (6:1b), neither of those points is mentioned in Mark. The clear impression of the Greek is that the plucking was part of their making their way through the field (literally, "and his disciples began to make a path by plucking the grain"; most modern translations of Mark 2:23b reflect the influence of the formulations in Matthew and Luke). Therefore, while the point of the story in Matthew and Luke is the comparison of the activity of David and his followers when they were hungry with Jesus' followers when they were hungry, that is not the case in Mark. Further, Jesus' defense in Matthew and Luke points out that even David and his followers broke the law when they were hungry, just as Jesus' followers did, thus citing a legal precedent for the disciples' action (e.g., necessity supersedes the law). That is not the point in Mark. As the Markan story is constructed, the comparison is not between hunger and hunger, since Mark says nothing about the disciples being hungry. Rather, the comparison is between David and Jesus. The point is thus christological: Jesus is to be permitted the same latitude of behavior as was David, God's chosen and anointed. Therefore, to understand, or even to translate, Mark's story in the light of the modifications it experienced in its inclusion in the later Gospels of Matthew and Luke, is to miss the point Mark is trying to make with his formulation of the tradition. Instead of a defense based on legal precedent, which the story became in Luke and Matthew, the defense in Mark is predicated on the status of Jesus, which is comparable with that of David. That the emphasis lies here in Mark, and not on the legal precedents of the OT account, is further indicated by the fact that Mark could allow to stand in his story an inaccurate statement about who the high priest was (2:26; a glance at 1 Sam. 22:20 will show Abiathar was not the priest at all). If Mark wanted to base Jesus' defense on legal precedent, such an instance of ignorance of the actual account would seriously compromise his case. Matthew and Luke, on the other hand, constructing a legal defense, corrected the error by omitting that incorrect reference.

Therefore, to understand the Markan account in the light of its later interpretation by Matthew and Luke will result in missing the point Mark seeks to make in the way he has used his traditions, as this example shows. Our task in these pages, therefore, will require us to take care to examine what Mark is saying, apart from the interpretation those same stories received in the Gospels written by Matthew and Luke.

In summary, what we face in the Gospel of Mark is a new literary attempt within the Christian community, and perhaps within the literature of the Hellenistic world, to say something about Jesus of Nazareth. It would be difficult to overestimate the importance of this new attempt, since the entire history of the Christian movement has been enormously influenced by the gospel literature. But it would also be difficult to overestimate the theological capacity of that unknown Christian who first conceived the idea of putting the hitherto unconnected traditions about Jesus into a larger framework. There was a time, now deservedly ended, when the author of the Gospel of Mark was regarded as rather dull-witted, allowing as he did so many uneven and awkward transitions, and so many unresolved tensions, to survive in his final product. Further study of that earliest Gospel has revealed it to be the product of an enormously subtle and sophisticated theological mind which faced and resolved the problem of combining a wide variety of independent, at times dissonant, pieces of tradition into a unified whole.

To enter the realm of Markan studies is therefore to enter into the excitement of new insights and fresh discoveries, as scholars seek not only to think Mark's thoughts after him, but to probe his narrative to gain some insight into the problems he sought to solve, and the resources he had available to him. It is to a discussion of that ongoing task that the following pages will be devoted. In them we will seek, as it were, to look over the author's shoulder as he writes his Gospel, attempting to discern something of the shape of the traditions which Mark had at his disposal, and something of the ways in which he used and adapted those traditions. We will then seek to trace out some of the major theological motifs that emerge from careful scrutiny of this pioneer literary work. We will attempt, in short, to understand something of the method and the goals pursued by that unknown theological genius of the primitive church, who gave to the traditions about Jesus a shape and an interpretation to which we owe, in large measure, the present contours of the Christian understanding of Jesus of Nazareth.

CHAPTER TWO

Purpose
Theology

THE INTENTION OF MARK'S GOSPEL

It is not difficult, in reading the Gospels, to get the impression that they intend to give the reader a sequentially accurate picture of the history of Jesus. That remains up to the present the understanding that many people bring to their reading of these documents of the primitive church. Such an assumption about the Gospels presupposes that one can trace the development of Jesus' thought by following the sequence of the stories in the various Gospels, filling in with creative imagination the psychological motivations which must have been present to account for the course Jesus' career took, and the way he taught and preached. If one does that carefully enough, there seems to be a good chance that one can achieve an understanding of what motivated Jesus to do what he did, and how he reacted to the various forces that were arrayed against him. One can suppose, for example, that the structure of Mark represents Jesus' attempt to go to the masses of people (chaps. 1–8) with his proclamation of the kingdom of God. Disappointed with their uncomprehending reaction and the disciples' as well, he decided to devote himself to teaching those disciples (chaps. 9–13) so that his inevitable death would at least leave them prepared to carry on. A variation often introduced is the idea that Jesus, finding no success that pleased him in his Galilean ministry, decided he must confront the opposition in its home base, Jerusalem, perhaps with the intention of dying there, or perhaps simply to have a "showdown" with the religious authorities of Judaism.

Any such attempt inevitably reveals gaps in the narrative of any one of the Gospels, especially Mark, so the other Gospels are used to fill in the gaps where that can be done. Furthermore, because it is easier to fit the one-year ministry of the synoptics into the three-year scheme of John rather than the other way around, a history of Jesus' three-year ministry is usually constructed, with the content and order coming largely from the synoptics. Even though the three-year scheme in John, for example, puts the cleansing of the temple as one of the earliest acts of Jesus' public ministry, (John 2:13–22), this event is regularly understood as coming during the final days of Jesus' life, as it is presented in the synoptics.

The resulting construction of the career of Jesus obviously does not really follow the account of any of the Gospels, but picks and chooses those elements which to the modern student seem most reasonable and appropriate. But such "picking and choosing" is inevitably governed more by the understanding and intention of the modern student than by the gospel materials themselves, since the need for such selectivity and careful supplementation clearly shows the inadequacy of any one Gospel, or all of them together, for such an attempt. It was this discovery, namely, that the construction of a career of Jesus from the Gospels owed more to the scholar's preconceptions about Jesus than it did to any "objective" history which could be distilled from the Gospel accounts, that brought to an end the attempt to write a "life of Jesus" which had dominated late nineteenth and early twentieth century NT scholarship. Albert Schweitzer's book *The Quest of the Historical Jesus* with its summary of all such attempts up to the time he wrote his book (1906) made that point clear.

A careful scrutiny of the Gospels makes clear that the resources for such historical reconstruction simply are not present. What appears to be historical narrative in Matthew or Luke is simply the result, in many instances, of attempts to resolve ambiguities in the Markan narrative, which they used as one of their sources. For example, in Mark's account of the calling of Levi (2:13–17), it is not at all clear in the Greek whose house provided the scene of the ensuing meal, Levi's or Jesus' (that Jesus had a home in Capernaum according to Mark's narrative is clear from 2:1). Mark 2:15 simply says it occurred in "his house," without being clear as to the antecedent of the possessive pronoun. When Luke took over this part of Mark's narrative, he clarified the ambiguity; in Luke 5:29, it is now clear that the meal was in *Levi's* house. In addition, the discussion about fasting, which in Mark is not integrated into the narrative (2:18–22), in Luke's hands became a further incident at that same meal (Luke 5:33–39). Thus, the clear historical impression given by the Lukan narrative is due, not to better historical information Luke had, but to his desire to eliminate some ambiguities in Mark's narrative. The resulting account in Luke is thus due to literary polishing, not historical accuracy.

A careful scrutiny of Mark's narrative also reveals insurmountable problems for any attempt to recreate a sequentially accurate account of Jesus' career. Any attempt, for example, even to give a geographical account of Jesus' itinerary will come to grief within the Markan narrative. For example, in Mark 6:45 Jesus commands his disciples to go across the Sea of Galilee to Bethsaida while he remains behind to dismiss the crowds. Following the ensuing storm and Jesus' entry into the boat after he has come to them walking on the water, Mark informs us they landed at Gennesaret. Any attempt to explain the discrepancy (the wind blew them off course; Jesus gave new instructions after he got into the boat; they went on from Bethsaida to Gennesaret) is based entirely on non-Markan guesses. There is no way to solve the problem from the narrative. Again, the geographical information in Mark 7:31 is strange, to say the least; so strange, in fact, that translators regularly change the intention of Mark's language. Not only is Sidon north of Tyre, so that returning south to Galilee by going north through Sidon makes little sense, but the Sea of Galilee is not "in the midst" of the Decapolis, as Mark's Greek clearly states (the translation "through the region of the Decapolis" is an attempt to "save" Mark from the impossibility of his own language). Such geographical information simply cannot be included in an itinerary of Jesus because it is contrary to geographical reality. Again, Mark uses language in his accounts of Jesus' crossings of the Sea of Galilee that have Jesus making successive journeys from west to east without any mention of a return, either by sea or land (4:35 and 5:1; 5:31). The Greek phrase used (*eis to peran*) normally means to go from the area of Palestine, which lies to the west of the Sea of Galilee and the Jordan River, to the land lying to the east of sea and river. Any attempt to straighten out this problem will again owe more to the imagination of the one who solves the problem than it will to Mark's text. That it was in fact a problem is shown by the way the other two Gospels corrected Mark's language. While both Matthew and Luke reproduce the first *eis to peran* (Matt. 8:18, although he has inserted some other material between the command in v. 18 and its execution in v. 23; Luke 8:22), neither of them reproduces the second one in Mark 5:21. Matthew omits that material altogether, while Luke changes the *eis to peran* to *hypostrephein*, a word meaning "return," thus eliminating the problem of consecutive voyages from west to east shore. Clearly, then, the Markan framework is incapable of providing the information necessary to recreate Jesus' historical itinerary, and the more historical appearance of that itinerary in Matthew and Luke is due to their attempts to clarify one of their literary sources. They are apparently as dependent on Mark as we are for an outline of Jesus' itinerary.

We will fare no better if we try to reconstruct a chronological sequence from Mark's narrative framework. Let one example suffice. We learn in 4:35 that Jesus and his disciples set out across the Sea of Galilee "when evening had come." Before we hear again of any chronological reference ("on the Sabbath," 6:2), Jesus crossed the Sea of Galilee and stilled its storm, healed the Gerasene demoniac, made another trip across the sea, healed the woman with the flow of blood, went to Jairus' house and raised his daughter from the dead, and returned "to his own country." If we are meant to think that the day following the evening of 4:35 was the sabbath of 6:2, then all those events recited occurred at night, a patent absurdity. Yet any attempt to say that a longer period of time was envisioned will find no support whatsoever within the text of Mark. The alternatives we face are: either follow the text, which leads to absurdity, or leave the text, which is to admit that the text will not provide us with a sequentially accurate chronology.

It is precisely this kind of discovery about the nature of the Markan framework which led scholars, operating some decades ago, to conclude that Mark could not have been a very clever person, since he allowed such discrepancies to enter his narrative. That is true if Mark's intention were to write history. If, however, Mark is pursuing another purpose with the way he arranged his narrative, then the question of history simply misses Mark's point. In fact, that is at present the scholarly consensus about the order in which Mark put his narrative about Jesus. Mark has arranged his material in the way he has, not to make a historical point, but to make a theological one. If the intention of Mark is thus theological, not historical, then any historical or geographic references are much more likely to serve theological than historical intentions. To read Mark as a historical narrative is to misread him. What we must find is the theological point that caused him to arrange his materials in the way he did. It is just this attempt that has occupied, and continues to occupy, many of the scholars who are presently concerning themselves with Mark.

What all of that means is simply this: we cannot move from the present shape of Mark's narrative to conclusions about the history of Jesus with any hope of arriving at historically reliable results. That is due to the fact that the Markan narrative in its present form exists at least two stages removed from the historical events themselves. This point can be clarified by speaking of three "levels" or "kinds" of material in relation to the Gospel of Mark as we now have it.

In such a scheme, the first "level" would be the present form of the Gospel of Mark. (This discussion would also hold true of the other Gospels, but we will limit ourselves here to discussing Mark.) This level represents the final form given to the material by the final author, and it embodies his intentions for, and understanding of, the materials he has incorporated into the Gospel. It represents, therefore, the expression of his theological understanding of the significance of Jesus of Nazareth. Scholars now feel that the differences between the various Gospels are due to the differing theological concepts which informed the way they used and arranged the material. One of the ways to determine just what those theological concepts were is to compare the way in which Gospel authors used and adapted the material they had available. Adaptations will show the kind of theology underlying such changes. This method, called "redaction-history" or "-criticism," obviously is most effective when we can compare the edited, adapted form with the original source. For that reason, the surest results gained by employing this method are achieved in regard to Matthew and Luke, since we also possess one of their sources, viz., Mark. Since we do not possess the sources that Mark and John used, we must attempt by literary analysis to disentangle the sources which now lie embedded in their narratives and then reconstruct them. This is obviously a difficult task, and scholars are only beginning to undertake it. There are, however, other ways to infer Mark's theological intentions. A careful examination of recurring patterns in his narrative, for example, would point to an important concern. A study of characteristic Markan language, his style and vocabulary, will also aid us in isolating those portions of his narrative where his own work is most heavily concentrated. Those portions, in turn, ought to betray some, at least, of the theological intentions embodied in the narrative he wrote. In this way, it is possible to detect the kind of theological outlook the evangelist brought to his task, which in turn shaped the way he adapted and arranged his material.

A second "level" of material is represented by the traditions and the tradition-complexes available to the Gospel authors. Analysis of the Gospel of Mark has made clear that Mark combined different kinds of traditions that had circulated before he wrote his Gospel. Often the shape of these traditions can still be seen even though they are now embedded in Mark's narrative. These "forms" can be described and catalogued, and then inferences can be drawn about the kind of theology they represented, and what kind of need they filled in the preaching and teaching of the primitive church in the time before the Gospels were written. This kind of analysis is called "form-criticism" or "-history." We can recognize, for instance, a form that little "anecdotes" about Jesus regularly have. Such a story, for example, as Mark 2:23–28 describes a situation (v. 23), a reaction to that situation by a class of people, or someone who represents a class (v. 24), and then Jesus' response to that situation (vv. 25–26). A kind of generalizing conclusion may also be attached (vv. 27–28). This kind of anecdote is found again and again in Mark, sometimes in just this form, sometimes with added dialogue included within Jesus' response. Another kind of story is found in Mark 1:30–31, where a "problem" is stated (v. 30), a "solution" is reported (v. 31a), and a "proof" is given that indicates the problem really has been solved (v. 31b). That is the basic outline miracle stories follow, often with expanded detail in any one of the three steps within the story. Characteristically, such kinds of stories are "rounded off." That is, they can be understood quite apart from the context in which they now stand; in some instances, the present context does not help in understanding them at all. Their existence prior to the gospel narratives is thus clearly attested: they were framed to be understood as independent units, apart from any kind of context of the life of Jesus.

Again, sayings of Jesus will be given with no indication of their original context. An example of such a series of sayings is found in Mark 4:21–22, 24–25. The fact that they do not depend on their

Markan context for their meaning is indicated by the way in which Matthew and Luke used them. All four verses are included in both Matthew and Luke, but each of them in a different place: Mark 4:21 is found in Matt. 5:15 and Luke 11:33; Mark 4:22 in Matt. 10:26 and Luke 8:17, and so on. Clearly, such sayings can have meaning in a variety of contexts, and are thus bound to no specific context.

The recurrence of such clearly structured forms indicates that this material had circulated long enough orally to be refined to that form which was best remembered, and that, more importantly, made the point the material was intended to make. Obviously, the analysis of the material at this "second level" will lack the certainty of the results obtained at the first or redactional level, because we have nothing against which to test the results of this form-critical analysis. The only stories we have that circulated orally are either embedded in the Gospels themselves, or occur in writings of the early church fathers. In the latter case, we can never be sure whether the fathers are citing gospel material from memory, or from a different version of our Gospels, or from oral tradition that continued on after the Gospels were written. For that reason they do not provide the kind of objective check on the results of form-critical analysis that is provided on the first "level" when the present form of Mark can be compared with the use made of it by Matthew or Luke. The important point on this "level" of material is this: the forms in which it is cast are literary forms, and one must reckon here with a period of time during which such forms developed. What this material will therefore reflect in the first instance will be the theological understanding of the primitive church within which this material circulated, and within which it achieved its present form. Even at this level, one is not yet dealing with actual "historical" events or narrative.

Such material can be approached only on the third "level," the level of the actual historical events that gave rise to the traditions (second level) which are embodied in the Gospels (first level). Obviously, the results of investigations at this level will be the most tentative of all, since the only indicators we have of these events are the pieces of tradition we have disentangled from their present position in the Gospels, and have analysed as to their probable form and function in the pre-Gospel level. We must therefore be very cautious in making positive statements about the historical events in the career of Jesus, since those events must be disentangled from the theological motifs embodied in the pre-Gospel tradition. No non-Gospel materials about Jesus have proved to be of any significance at all in the recovery of his historical career. If we are to locate that history, it must be from the materials now embedded in the Gospels.

As we have already indicated, such history will not be found in the order and structure of the whole narrative. We have already seen that the framework of the earliest Gospel, Mark, will not provide, and does not intend to provide, such information. We will have to derive it from the individual units of pre-Gospel traditions. But this material has already been shaped by the desire to make a theological point. Only when we can be sure that we have discounted that theological point can we begin to speak about "historical" results. How is such a task to be undertaken?

One step will have to be the recognition of the theological tendency at work in shaping the material. If the material in question, a saying, or the report of a deed of Jesus, represents a theological tendency we know was at work in the primitive church, we will have to suspect that the material itself was shaped (if it was not originated) by the primitive church to such an extent that the underlying event can no longer be discovered. Only if the material is dissimilar to such theological tendencies can we attribute historical reality to it with some degree of confidence. On the other hand, we know that Jesus aroused the enmity of the religious leaders of the Jews to the extent that he was executed with their active involvement and cooperation. Thus, any material that would be quite acceptable to the Jewish outlook of that time will also have to be called into question, so far as its historical value is concerned, since if in fact Jesus did act that way, the Jewish and Roman authorities would have had no reason to want to see him eliminated.

This kind of reasoning has led scholars to speak of the criteria of "dissimilarity" which must be applied when we seek to reach reliable information on the third, or historical "level." Once such material is established, other criteria may be applied, such as the criterion of multiple attestation (does the material appear in more than one source?, e.g., Mark, "Q," etc.); or the criterion of coherence (does the material thus derived hang together in some kind of coherent pattern?). None of these approaches will yield complete certainty.

Indeed, the result of a conscientious application of the criteria of dissimilarity would be a non-Jewish Jesus who bore no relationship in what he said or did to those who set out to follow him. Such a caricature need not result, however, if the methods are applied with care. Let us look briefly at an example of the way historical material may be derived from the material as it now appears in our Gospel.

We will use as our example Mark 12:28–34. Its understanding does not depend on its present context, i.e., within the temple, close to the time of Jesus' arrest and death. It could be placed at any point in Jesus' career and it would be equally understandable, as Luke demonstrates by placing the story at a much earlier point in his account. It also shows signs of being "rounded off"; that is, it is a self-contained story that can be understood with no reference to its present context in the life of Jesus, or any other context, for that matter. Thus, apart from the first part of v. 28, and the last phrase of v. 34, which adapt it to the Markan narrative, the story belonged to the pre-Markan stage of tradition. Thus, we have moved from level one (Markan redaction: vv. 28b, 34b) to level two (pre-Markan tradition).

To move from level two to level three, the historical level, we must ask whether or not this story betrays any tendencies within the early church which would throw suspicion on the story as an attempt by the church to retroject its ideas onto the historical Jesus in order to justify them. Here we get a mixed reading. On the one hand, contrary to virtually all other passages in the synoptic Gospels, a scribe is placed in a positive light: he approves of what Jesus says (v. 32), and Jesus approves his answer (v. 34). The word "scribe" is used eighteen times in Mark, other than this passage, and each time in a negative or hostile setting toward Jesus. Such a view is also characteristic of the other Gospels. When Matthew and Luke took over this story from Mark, they changed the scribe's innocent question into an attempt to trap Jesus (Matt. 22:35; Luke 10:25), and both omit the scribe's positive repetition of what Jesus had said, as well as Jesus' positive response to the scribe. This story, therefore, apparently took its form before scribal enmity among Christians had hardened; the story surely does not represent Mark's usual view of scribes.

Furthermore, while the content of Jesus' saying about love of God and neighbor is very important for later Christian theology, it is not for Mark; the noun "love" (*agapē*) appears nowhere in his Gospel and the verbal form in only one other place (10:21). Thus, if it does not reflect a Markan tendency, the only way the later church could have influenced the story was to add it to Mark at a later time, but there is no evidence that Mark ever circulated without this story. From that point of view, the story has a claim to historicity.

On the other hand, such a question to a rabbi about the most important law was a common practice among Jews of Jesus' time, and the answer Jesus gives, quoting from the OT, surely does not fit the criterion of being dissimilar to Jewish thought and practice. Yet the answer of the scribe, particularly his denigration of temple worship (Mark 12:33b), would hardly make this story appropriate as an apologetic to Jewish beliefs on the part of the earliest Christians. As an apologetic justification for Christian practices regarding the temple, it would be more appropriate coming from Jesus than from a scribe.

Therefore, there is some reason to see underlying the present form of this story a historical event which the early followers of Jesus remembered, and which, in passing through the oral period of tradition, was given its present form, probably because it helped solve the problem of the meaning of the Jewish law for the Christian faith: its essence is love of God and neighbor.

All of this may seem the "long way around" to arrive at such tentative judgments about the historicity of an event recorded in the Gospels, but, given the nature of the Gospels and of the primitive faith, there is no alternative. This has many implications. Let us single out two. First, one should learn to be very careful not to assume that when dealing with level one (the redactional level, the present shape of the Gospel), one can make statements appropriate to level three (the historical level). A great deal of confusion has been generated among scholars and preachers who do that, and its avoidance would help both preacher and scholar remain truer to the intention of the material with which he is working. If the primary motivation of both levels one (redaction) and two (oral tradition) is theological, that fact ought to be honored in the way one uses this material. If the material is intended to answer theological rather than historical questions, then one ought to respect the material enough to address to it the appropriate questions.

Secondly, when using this material in preaching, one ought not try to imagine what went on in Jesus' mind at this time in the temple, and then use that as the key to interpreting, say, Jesus' positive reaction to the scribe (e.g., he had been attacked so relentlessly—Mark 12:13–27—that, finding a friendly attitude, he gratefully acknowledged it). Luke's willingness to use the story in another context shows the independence of the story from any specific locus in Jesus' life, and the arrangement of material in the temple is, as we shall see, appropriate to Mark's own theological understanding of Jesus. Thus, the context will tell us how *Mark* understood this event; it will tell us nothing at all about how *Jesus* understood and reacted to this event in its present, Markan context. That is true of all the gospel materials. The preacher ought not impose level three (historical) judgments on level one (redactional) materials. The only result from such imposition will be an interpretation that owes more to the interpreter than to the material. If the order of the material in Mark, as in the other Gospels, is due to the evangelist, one ought to respect that fact, and not assume the right to speculate on the meaning of those events as though their order reflected the actual historical sequence of Jesus' life. There is theology enough in any given passage from Mark to occupy the preacher; there is no need to import a dubious historicity into a narrative that is shaped around other interests.

In summary, we have seen something of the nature of the intention of the Markan Gospel: it is proclamation rather than history. We have traced the material Mark arranged through its three "levels," and have seen something of the history of this material as it made its way through the primitive community to its present shape in Mark's Gospel. We must now take a more detailed, careful look at the ways in which Mark shaped and arranged the materials at his disposal.

CHAPTER THREE

MARK'S METHOD OF
CREATING A NARRATIVE

If, as we have reason to believe, the kind of literature we know as a "gospel" did not exist prior to Mark, then the composition of such a narrative in itself represents a significant attempt to achieve a new way of interpreting the Jesus traditions. Up to that time, those traditions could apparently be adequately interpreted by adapting and re-adapting them individually. Mark, on the other hand, apparently felt that method was no longer adequate to insure the kind of interpretation of the Jesus traditions he now saw to be necessary. The time had come for the individual traditions to be placed under the control of an overall interpretation of the career of Jesus of Nazareth. For that, Mark apparently felt a narrative framework was necessary, within which those traditions could be used in the service of that larger interpretation.

One way of achieving such an interpretation lay in the arrangement in which those individual stories were placed. If, as we saw earlier, most of the stories and sayings contained in Mark's Gospel had, up to that time, circulated within the primitive Christian communities with no specific context attached to them, then the author of our earliest Gospel had a considerable amount of freedom with respect to the way he could arrange those traditions. Careful consideration of the order in which the stories appear will therefore aid us in interpreting this Gospel.

A second method Mark used in his attempt to make those traditions useful for the longer narrative he had in mind was to shape the individual traditions themselves so they could function as part of his longer story, rather than simply as individual units. A detailed examination of the individual stories will frequently reveal how such shaping took place, and will thus give us further clues concerning how Mark intended his narrative to be understood. A third method Mark adopted in order to provide some kind of continuity for his narrative, and in order to give to that narrative the kind of meaning he wanted it to bear was to compose short summaries and interpretative comments, which he then placed at strategic points in his narrative. Careful attention to these compositions by our Gospel author himself will therefore reveal further clues to the meaning of his Gospel.

The task which will occupy us in the following pages will be an examination of these methods, in order to see just how Mark used them. Once we have seen examples of the way Mark composed his Gospel from the earlier Jesus traditions, we will be in a better position to ask about the meaning of the overall structure he achieved by means of those methods.

We will consider first the way Mark shaped his narrative by the arrangement he gave to the traditions he used. By juxtaposing traditions to one another, he was able to allow them to interpret each other in such a way that made further comment unnecessary, or so at least he seems to have thought. Perhaps his conservative bent over against the earlier Jesus traditions made this manner of interpretation seem preferable to rewriting those traditions. For whatever reason, however, much of what Mark wanted to say, he said by means of the way he ordered the traditions at his disposal. An example will show the kind of interpretation Mark could achieve by means of such a juxtaposition of traditions.

Among the events Mark narrates during Jesus' final visit to Jerusalem are the cleansing of the temple and the cursing of a fig tree (11:12–25). Mark has taken the account of the cleansing of the temple and bracketed it with the story of the cursing of the fig tree, in that way clearly indicating that he intends the two stories to be understood in relationship to one another. Taken by itself, there are some problems within the story of the cursing of the fig tree. It seems to put Jesus in questionable light, as one who takes out his frustration on a tree when the fruit he sought from it was not to be found. To add to the problem, there is the strange statement that the tree bore nothing more than leaves because it was not the time for figs (v. 13). That makes Jesus' cursing the tree all the more unreasonable. Why curse a tree for not producing fruit out of its normal time? The conclusion of the account has appended to it some sayings about faith (vv. 22–24) and prayer (vv. 24–25), themes which characterize neither the story of the fig tree nor the account of the temple cleansing. Either such elements are introduced because of the total interpretative intent of Mark in this arrangement of tradition, or Mark was, as it was once fashionable to conclude, somewhat muddled.

The story of the cleansing of the temple also has more far-reaching implications, as Mark presents it, than have always been realized. The attack on the money-changers and the merchants is far more important than simply an indication of Jesus' pique at such activity within the temple precincts, or his indignation at dishonest business practices, of which there is not a word in the text. Rather, by this act of prophetic protest, Jesus demonstrated that the practices necessary for the normal functioning of the temple must come to an end. If sacrificial animals cannot be purchased, then the sacrifice cannot be carried on. If money proper for the paying of the half-sheckel temple tax can not be obtained, the monetary support of the temple and its priesthood would have to come to an end. If no vessels (the Greek word is frequently used in the Greek version of the OT to mean the sacred temple vessels) can be moved within the temple (there is no hint that Mark means us to understand the prohibition to apply only to the outer court, the "Court of the Gentiles"), then all activity relating to the normal cultic celebrations within the temple must cease.

The reference from Jeremiah to the temple as a "den of robbers" does not refer to dishonest practices within the temple walls. The robbers' cave is the place of retreat *after* the robbers have committed their crimes (cf. Jer. 7:8–11). The brunt of the accusation thus concerns the use to which the temple is put: people think so long as the temple services are continued, they may retreat there, no matter how they have acted outside its walls, and still find forgiveness and fellowship with God. It is this kind of attitude that the tradition of the temple cleansing in Mark indicates as the motive for Jesus' act. Because the temple of God is abused in that way, it has ceased to have any point. Finally, only in the Markan tradition are the words "for all nations" included in the quotation from Isa. 56:7: "My house shall be called a house of prayer for all nations."

As the tradition is found in Mark, therefore, the temple cleansing represents Jesus' prophetic–symbolic act of ending cultic worship within the temple, because it has been abused on the assumption that the temple cult made forgiveness for any kind of behavior automatic, and because the necessary universal worship of God, to be centered in the temple, simply had not come about. It is precisely that point that Mark wants to reinforce by combining the traditions of the cursing of the fig tree and the cleansing of the temple.

The fig tree which has not borne its proper fruit, and which has therefore been cursed, is symbolic of the temple which, by Jesus' actions within it, Jesus similarly "cursed." The effectiveness of the curse of the fig tree, noted after the cleansing of the temple, makes clear that the temple, too, will ultimately be destroyed, a point that is later made explicitly by Jesus (13:2), and which figures in his trial (14:58) and in the derision that accompanies his crucifixion (15:29). With his death, the temple is symbolically destroyed (15:38), as it will finally be physically destroyed in AD 70 by the Romans. In that way, Mark uses the story of the fig tree to interpret the significance of Jesus' prophetic symbolism in his activity within the temple: the fate of the fig tree will be the fate of the temple. Jesus has "cursed" it. It will "die."

The desire to interpret the significance of Jesus' actions in the temple probably also accounts for the remark about the "time for figs" and the inclusion of the reference to "all nations" with respect to the purpose of the temple. It is clear in Mark that the inclusion of the gentiles in the salvation Jesus announces (the "kingdom of God") is part of God's plan. Jesus, according to Mark, travels outside the boundaries of "Jewish" areas (e.g., 7:24, 31; 8:27) and in the "little apocalypse" in Mark 13 specifically states that the gospel being preached to "all nations" (or "all gentiles"; the Greek word is the same) is a precondition for the consummation of the kingdom of God (13:10). This priority of evangelistic activity among the gentiles is strongly reminiscent of a tradition we also find in Paul, where the inclusion of the "full number" of gentiles is a precondition for the conversion of Israel, and the final consummation (Rom. 11:25–26a). If that is the case, then, according to God's plan, the temple, because it did not include gentiles among its worshipers, cannot play any further role. What Jesus sought in the temple—inclusion of "all nations" in the prayers spoken there—was absent. In fact, according to God's plan, the temple in its present configuration could not fulfill that plan; for Mark, proclamation to the gentiles will only begin after Jesus' death. Thus, when Jesus destroys temple worship, he symbolically announces that God has no further use for it; Jesus, not the temple, is now the locus for finding God. Therefore, as it was not "time for figs," it was not time for the consummation in the temple. This also explains why sayings about faith and prayer are an appropriate way to conclude this complex of traditions. That Mark assembled them here is clear when we notice that both Matthew and Luke felt free to put some or all of them in other contexts or omit them entirely; perhaps they know from other sources that these sayings were originally independent. What Mark means to say by this conclusion is simply that the locus of salvation, of God's plan, has shifted from temple to Jesus, and that therefore faith and prayer, not temple cults, are the way to God. That "faith" for Mark can only be understood in relation to Jesus is clear from the opening summary of Jesus' preaching in Mark: repent, and have faith in the gospel (1:15; as we shall see, "gospel" means Jesus and his career).

Mark, by the arrangement of the traditions of the cursing of the fig tree and the cleansing of the temple, intends them to interpret each other, and thus to make a point he wants to emphasize about the importance of Jesus over against the historic importance of temple worship within Jewish religious life. Such arrangement of traditions is, as we noted earlier, a favorite device of Mark, a point to which we shall return in subsequent discussions. What that means to one who seeks to understand the intention of Mark's witness to the importance of Jesus, his words and acts, is clear: one must pay very careful attention to the *arrangement* of those earlier traditions. Such arrangements and juxtapositions constitute a major hermeneutical device of the author of this earliest Gospel, and careful attention to them is an indispensable aid in understanding that Gospel. In the following chapters, we shall have recourse again and again to noting the importance of the ordering of traditions in Mark when we seek to understand some of the major theological motifs which inform Mark's Gospel.

A second way in which Mark interpreted the traditions he used was by adapting them rather than simply by arranging or juxtaposing them. Such adaptation can take the form of providing a tradition with an introduction, a conclusion (or both), or by including several individual traditions in a larger narrative unit. We will examine those devices in that order.

An example of adapting traditions by providing an introduction to them, thus integrating them into a larger unity, can be found in the geographical notations in Mark 7:24 and 31. V. 24 introduces the story of the healing of the daughter of the Syrophoenician woman with the information that Jesus has left Galilee (the last geographical reference was to Gennesaret, 6:53) and has gone to the region of Tyre and Sidon. There is indication within the story itself that it circulated originally apart from such a geographical notation. For example, the woman is identified as a "Syrophoenician" (v. 26). But what is so unusual about that, since Jesus was in the region of Syrophoenicia? What other kind of woman would one expect to live there? Furthermore, Jesus' reference to the need first to feed the children is strange in view of the fact that Jesus has taken the "bread" (here it would mean his healing ministry) from the "children" (the Jews) into the region of the "dogs" (gentiles). He has come to her region; why should the woman not expect him to be willing to help her? If, on the other hand, the story were originally understood to have concerned an event that occurred in Galilee, the identification of the woman would be necessary for the story (she would then be the foreigner, not Jesus, as in the present setting), and her initiative in coming to Jesus would make sense of the ensuing conversation. As we have already seen, the geographically confused information contained in 7:31, which is clearly meant to follow on the information contained in v. 24, cannot have referred to an actual journey. It is best explained as an attempt to construct an itinerary for Jesus in a non-Jewish area, a construction attempted by one whose knowledge of that part of the eastern Mediterranean world is less than exact (a point that will have some importance later when we ask about the author of this Gospel).

Thus, vv. 24 and 31 have been used by Mark to introduce two traditions and combine them in such a way that they now become a short excursion of Jesus beyond the area of Jewish territory. There is some likelihood that Mark in that way sought to give justification to later Christian missionary enterprises to areas other than the Jewish homelands. It is also very likely that Mark is responsible for most introductions to traditions which place those traditions in some specific location, whether beside the sea (2:13), at home in Capernaum (2:1), or some other, similar location.

A similar method of adapting a tradition is to provide it with a conclusion. For example, the story of Jesus and his disciples passing through a grainfield on the sabbath has had added to it by Mark another saying of Jesus about the sabbath (2:27–28). In that way, the general point of the story—Jesus is free to do as he pleases on the sabbath, as are his followers—is made clear: Jesus can act in this way because of the inherent importance of his person. He is, as the Son of man (we will return to this title in a later chapter), Lord over the sabbath. Hints that this is a conclusion provided by Mark are found in the fact that the story is quite complete without it: Jesus has made his defense in a sufficient manner in vv. 25–26. Furthermore, the saying, which itself can be understood apart from its attachment to this story, is affixed to the story by a phrase which, as scholars have long recognized, is a Markan attachment formula: "and he said to them" (*kai elegen autois*).

Mark is also capable of providing a story with both introduction and conclusion, as is probably the case with the account of Jesus' first exorcism (1:21–28). Here Mark has taken a story of Jesus casting out a demon (vv. 23–26) and has framed it by providing an introduction (vv. 21–22) and a conclusion (vv. 27–28) which turn the point of the story from an account of Jesus' power as an exorcist into an account of the power and novelty of Jesus as a teacher. We will want to return to this story again at a later point to examine the importance and implications of such an adaptation.

A further way of adapting traditions, which Mark employs with some frequency, consists in combining more than one independent tradition into a matrix which transforms the result into a larger narrative unit. There is considerable evidence, for example, that the present shape of Mark 6:1–6 is due in large measure to the editorial activity of Mark. The saying about the unacceptability of a prophet among his own kinfolk is attributed to Jesus, independently of this context, in two non-canonical collections of the sayings of Jesus (*Coptic Gospel of Thomas*, saying 31; *Oxyrhynchus Papyrus* I, lines 31–36), clear evidence that it circulated simply as a saying. The fact that it is again introduced by the Markan attachment formula (*kai elegen autois*, v. 4) is further confirmation that Mark found it in that form and has included it here. The saying in *Coptic Thomas* and *Papyrus Oxyrhynchus* has a second half: to "No prophet is acceptable in his village" is added: "No physician works cures on those who know him." Mark has apparently chosen to transform the second half of the saying into narrative (v. 5) and then concludes the whole as an example of unbelief among those who knew Jesus best (v. 6a). The first two verses of this account also contain language that consistently recurs in what scholars recognize as Markan introductions, showing that in all probability Mark has formulated them as introduction to the unit. Finally, it is interesting that only the phrase at the end of v. 3, and the material Mark then attaches, gives a negative cast to the reaction of the people described in vv. 2b–3a. Otherwise, the astonishment of the people and their remarks about his teaching need no more be seen negatively than the very similar reaction to his teaching in 1:27–28. Perhaps Mark found an independent tradition recounting Jesus' reception by his amazed townsfolk, and, knowing that some of them rejected him (cf. 3:20–21, 31–35), included the tradition here within this different context. Placed at this point in the narrative, it prepares us, as did 3:20–35, along with much other material, for Jesus' final rejection by his kinsfolk, the Jews. In that way, Mark took two originally independent, unrelated traditions about Jesus, and by providing a narrative matrix adapted those traditions to make a theological point about Jesus' ultimate fate.

A third way, in addition to juxtaposition of traditions and adaptation by means of which Mark interpreted the Jesus tradition, was the composition of summaries of varying length, which he interspersed throughout the early chapters of his Gospel. Such summaries can be recognized by the fact that they contain typically Markan language, but more importantly, perhaps, by the fact that they presuppose their present location in the narrative to be understood. They are not "rounded off," that is, they do not show any sign that they circulated independently prior to their inclusion in Mark, and they presuppose the information one has already received from the Markan narrative up to the point of their inclusion. For example, the material in 8:19–21, where Jesus questions the disciples about the wondrous feedings of the multitudes, supposes not only that the two feedings already narrated in Mark have occurred (6:35–44; 8:1–10), but also presupposes the actual Greek form of those narratives. The two narratives of the feedings use different words for "basket"; that difference is accurately reflected in Jesus' questions where the Greek word for basket in 8:19 corresponds to the word in 6:43, and another Greek word for basket, used in 8:20, corresponds to the word in 8:8. That summary, therefore, presupposes not only the present order of events in Mark, but also the present form of the Greek prose. Mark has thus composed this narrative-summary, calling attention to the importance of certain events he has already narrated. Other summaries can be found in 1:32–34; 2:13; 3:7–12 (although there may be some traditional materials incorporated in this longer summary, they have been rewritten by Mark to conform to his purpose here) and 6:54–56. Such summaries make clear to us that Mark is selecting only a few instances from Jesus' career to report in detail. He did much more healing and teaching than Mark's specific instances would indicate apparently, and Mark wants us to know that. He also wants his readers to know that Jesus' reputation was not limited to the immediate geographic area within which he moved. Jesus was known far and wide, and was regularly accompanied by large crowds who came to see and hear him. Again and again, introductory materials that Mark provides for the traditions he uses make those points (cf. 4:1–2 and 6:30–34 as only two more examples).

In such ways, then, Mark used the traditions available to him in his story about Jesus of Nazareth. By arranging, framing, and shaping traditions, he adapted them to fit into the larger story he wanted to tell. He also included in his narrative from time to time little compositions of his own, designed to point the reader beyond the limited impression created by his necessarily restricted account of individual acts of Jesus and individual teaching sessions. In those ways, Mark interpreted the traditions at his disposal to make them useful for the new way he wanted to present them—in the form of a running narrative about Jesus.

CHAPTER FOUR

THE STRUCTURE OF MARK

Our attempt to understand the theological intention that motivated Mark to undertake the kind of reinterpretation of the traditions about Jesus that the creation of a "gospel" represents, would take a long step forward if we could come to some clear understanding of the overall structure into which he placed the individual traditions. We have already gained some insight into his intention by examining the way he adapted those individual traditions, juxtaposing and framing them, and composing summaries. Further examination along such lines will yield further results. If, however, we could also plumb the theological motivation which underlies the overall structure of the Gospel, we would have a valuable cross-check on the results of our analyses of the smaller units within the Gospel.

The need to understand Mark's structure as a way of finding his theological intention is more acute in the case of Mark than it is in the case of Matthew and Luke. With the latter two, we are able to observe the way they handled their source-material, because we have one of those sources at our disposal, namely Mark. By seeing the way Matthew and Luke handled, adapted, and changed the material they take from Mark, we can make some highly plausible inferences about the theological motivations at work behind such changes. Unfortunately, we do not possess such a source for Mark. Attempts have been made to disentangle such sources from the present narrative of Mark's Gospel, with a view then to seeing how he used them, but such attempts by necessity share a degree of uncertainty which is not the case with Mark as the source for Matthew and Luke. We are therefore denied, in the case of Mark, some very significant clues to his theological purpose which we can easily obtain in the case of Matthew and Luke.

For that reason, a great deal of attention has been focused on the problem of interpreting and understanding the overall plan of Mark's Gospel. While there are certain structural elements within the overall plan that students of Mark have found and on which they can agree, there is as yet no unanimity on the structure or the outline of the Gospel of Mark. That is to say, there is as yet no consensus as to the theological motivation that caused Mark to arrange his material in the shape and order in which he did. It is the purpose of these next few pages to expose the present shape of the problem.

Perhaps the best place to start is with some of those structural characteristics of Mark which are fairly obvious and on which scholars can agree. For example, one of the structural features of Mark's Gospel consists in his bracketing one tradition with the two halves of another. We saw an example of that in the last chapter when we considered the stories of the withered fig tree and the cleansing of the temple. There, Mark has put the story about the temple into the middle of the story about Jesus cursing a fig tree. Another place Mark uses the same device is in 5:21–43 where he has taken the story of the raising of Jairus' daughter and into it has inserted the story of the woman with the flow of blood. That the stories were formed independently of one another is revealed by an analysis of the Greek style of the two stories. They differ markedly in the number and use of participles and in the length and complexity of sentence structure. It is clear that the same person did not reduce them both to writing. There is no certainty that they were not thus combined before Mark got them, but Mark's predilection for this way of using his sources would add weight to the argument that Mark is responsible for combining them. Another instance is found in 6:7–31 where the account of Jesus' sending out his disciples and their return brackets two traditions about Herod and John the Baptist. Still another instance is found in 3:20–35 where an account of some Pharisees who think Jesus is in league with the devil (there called "Beelzebul") is bracketed by accounts of the way Jesus was misunderstood by members of his family.

There are still some unresolved problems connected with this particular Markan structure, however. It is clear in the account of the temple that the bracketing material is meant to interpret the material that stands within. The cursed and withered fig tree makes clear that Jesus is not purging the temple so it can continue in more fitting service to God. The fig tree is not pruned so it can bear fruit; it dies. Similarly, the act in the temple is to be understood, Mark makes clear, as the announcement of its end as well. It is not that clear, on the other hand, how the inserted traditions are meant to be interpreted in the other instances we noted. Perhaps only a stylistic feature is intended: in chap. 3 perhaps the dispute gives Jesus' family time to arrive at the place where Jesus is; in chap. 5 the account of the healing of the woman gives time for Jairus' daughter to die; in chap. 6 the stories about John the Baptist and Herod give the disciples time to complete their mission. Yet, in this last instance John is clearly Jesus' forerunner, even in John's death (the point of 9:11–13). Perhaps Mark wants to hint in this arrangement that Jesus' death (prefigured in John's death) is connected to the missionary activity of his followers. The coupling of rejection of Jesus by family and religious authorities may be meant to foreshadow his final abandonment by all (see 14:50). Perhaps the point of the combination of the woman with the flow of blood and the healing of Jairus' daughter is the desire to link a story which speaks of faith (5:34) with a story where such mention is absent. It is difficult to be certain in these instances, however.

A second characteristic of the structure of Mark's Gospel is found in the pattern of public teaching to the masses (including the disciples) and private explanation to the disciples. That occurs in 4:1–12; 7:14–23; 9:14–29; 10:1–10; and 13:1–8. Obviously, Mark is trying to make some point about the superior opportunity of the disciples to understand what Jesus said and did, since they had the advantage of private instruction from Jesus himself. Yet, it is also clear from repeated references that the disciples did not really profit from that instruction. They miss the point of such private instruction (see 6:52; 8:21; and 9:32 as examples) and in the end, they all desert him. On the other hand, it was precisely the followers of Jesus with whom the traditions about the words and deeds of Jesus began. If they misunderstood so badly, how can Mark use those traditions and still have any hope of representing fairly the significance of this Jesus? Or did they, at some point more hinted at than stated, finally come to an understanding? If they did, does that have any significance about the way we come to understand Jesus? These are also questions raised by the structure of Mark.

A third characteristic of the structure of Mark's Gospel is a three-fold repetition of a pattern of traditions found in chaps. 8–10. The pattern begins with Jesus' prediction of his fate: he must suffer, die, and will then rise from the dead (8:31; 9:30–32; 10:33–34). The next tradition concerns, in some way, the fact that the disciples do not really understand Jesus. In 8:32–33 it is Peter who rebuked Jesus (and was rebuked in return) because Jesus said he must suffer. In 9:33–34 the disciples dispute about who is the greatest, apparently having missed the implication that Jesus' greatness lies in the humility of his impending death. In 10:35–41 it is James and John who ask for places of power in the kingdom, apparently not realizing that Jesus' glory cannot occur before he dies. The third element in the pattern consists in words of Jesus on the nature of discipleship: 8:34–38; 9:35–37; 10:42–45. To that point the pattern is clear: the realization that Jesus must suffer is either rejected or missed by the disciples, which prompts Jesus to say something explicit on the subject. But there is also a fourth element in the pattern. It is a tradition in which Jesus is shown to be different from, or have powers beyond those of, ordinary men. In 9:2–8 it is the story of the transfiguration; in 9:38–41 it is a discussion of the power of Jesus' name which allows others by its use to cast out demons; in 10:46–52 it is the story of the healing of blind Bartimaeus. Are these traditions also meant by Mark to be part of the recurring pattern? If so, what point do they make in the pattern? If not, why are they included in each instance at the end of the pattern?

The problem is complicated by a further consideration. Although not in any exclusive or unique sense, chaps. 8–10 concern themselves primarily with traditions relating to Jesus' teaching activity to the disciples and to others. Prior to that section, Jesus has been described mainly as miracle worker; after that section, Mark begins his narrative of Jesus' final week in Jerusalem. Furthermore, in the whole of Mark, there are only two stories in which Jesus cures blindness. They occur at 8:22–26 and 10:46–52 at the beginning and end of the section concerned to a great extent with Jesus' teaching activity. Is that accidental? Or is Mark trying to say something about what must happen before anyone can understand Jesus? Is this a variation on his narrative technique of bracketing one tradition with another in order to interpret the bracketed material—in this case instructions with traditions of healing the blind? If that were the case, then the second story of the blind healing would be unlikely to be part of the threefold pattern. But why then the presence of the other, somewhat similar stories after the first two instances of the pattern? Again, the resolution of such questions awaits further insight.

Those are some of the recurring structures in Mark's narrative, which, if we could understand fully the reasons for their presence, would aid us in our attempt to understand the overall intention of Mark's reinterpretation of the traditions about Jesus. It is not enough to recognize such partial patterns, however. What can we say about the overall structure? Until that problem is solved, difficulties will remain in our understanding of the theology of Mark's Gospel.

One broad pattern to which attention has been called concerns the title "Son of God." It appears first in the account of the baptism of Jesus by John (1:9–11), when a voice from heaven identified Jesus, in words taken from Ps. 2:7 and Isa. 42:1, as God's beloved son. It appears again in the account of the transfiguration, when a heavenly voice again identified Jesus as God's beloved son. It appears a third and, in Mark's narrative, final time at the moment of Jesus' death on the cross, when the centurion commanding the Roman troops who crucified Jesus identified him as God's son. This title appears therefore at the beginning, the midpoint, and the conclusion of Mark's narrative, and seems to be the christological frame around which the Gospel may be arranged.

There can be little doubt that because of the title's appearance in such important events in the Gospel, it is important for Mark, but the use of that designation in those stories is such that there is no evident attempt to make them parallel. The words of the heavenly voice differ in the accounts of baptism and transfiguration and the title itself is in fact only an inference. "Son of God" or "God's Son" does not appear in those accounts, only "my beloved son." There can be no doubt that Mark understood that voice to carry divine authority, so the inference that Jesus is being identified as Son of God is surely valid, but it remains just that, an inference, and not a specific title. The centurion's confession, while surely important in Mark's understanding of Jesus, is not given the emphasis in his narrative that the first two accounts receive. The centurion is one of a number of people who watch Jesus die (15:40–41) and his confession seems to share significance with the rending of the temple veil (15:38). Perhaps most important of all, the title Son of God is not limited to these three occasions. In fact, the only time Mark has included it in its full form (the definite article is missing from the centurion's confession), he has used it in a summary as the title by which the demons identify Jesus (3:11). Nor is that use accidental; the only other time the title appears in Mark it is also spoken by a demon, who uses it in the form "Son of the Most High God" (5:7). In both of these instances, the spirit that utters the cry is identified as "unclean." It is hard to imagine that Mark could have found in that title a key around which to build his narrative. That is not to deny the importance of any of the first three accounts mentioned (baptism, transfiguration, centurion's confession), but if the link that binds them—identification of Jesus as God's son—is not used in them in any distinct way, then they can hardly have formed the skeleton upon which Mark built the rest of his Gospel. Each story is surely important for Mark, but not as elements in his basic outline.

A second broad pattern which scholars have regularly pointed to centers on the tradition that also occupies the approximate midpoint in the narrative: Peter's confession (8:27–30). Could that position be accidental, or did Mark intend in some way that the center in length of his Gospel would also be the center of its understanding and thus the key? This question has frequently been answered in the affirmative in the course of Markan scholarship. At this point, so it is often argued, Jesus realized that his attempt to reach the masses had failed. Not even his closest disciples had really understood what he was talking about. At this point, therefore, Jesus abandoned his attempt to reach the masses with his proclamation about God's kingdom and devoted himself to the private instruction of his disciples. Only in that way could he get across to them the meaning of his career and its relationship to God's kingdom, so they could carry on after the death he now foresaw in the not too distant future. Not only did he abandon his miracle-punctuated attempt to evangelize the masses, he also abandoned the area in which he had sought to win them, namely Galilee. In 8:27 Jesus went beyond Galilee into the region around Caesarea Philippi to the north, and when he did return, he desired to keep it secret, so he could continue his instruction of the disciples (9:30–31a). This second phase of Jesus' ministry continued until he entered Jerusalem, was captured, tried, and put to death.

While such an outline makes sense of a good deal of the material Mark has arranged in his account, it fails to be satisfactory on several counts. For one thing, the assumption which often underlies such an outline is that it reflects the historical course of Jesus' career. We have already seen that such an assumption does not comport with the framework Mark has provided for his traditions, a framework which yields neither sequentially accurate geography nor chronology. That means that if this is the midpoint in the narrative, it is just that, and must justify itself in some other way than an appeal to the actual historical course of Jesus' career. Much of the evidence cited will not support the outline on those terms.

For one thing, it is simply not true that after this confession by Peter the crowds which surrounded Jesus in the earlier narrative disappeared, and Jesus devoted himself from then on to the private instruction of the disciples. Jesus teaches as much publicly, and is as surrounded by crowds, after the incident at Caesarea Philippi as before. He joins a public dispute between his disciples and others (9:14) and performs a public miracle (9:17–29). He preaches to crowds "as," says Mark, "his custom was" (10:1), teaches publicly in the temple (11:17; 12:1, 35, 38) as he earlier had taught in the synagogues (1:21, 39; 6:2) and beside the sea (4:1), and carries on debates with the religious officials of Judaism after Caesarea Philippi (12:13, 18) as he had before in Galilee (2:15, 23; 3:1). Furthermore, he taught his disciples in private both before (4:10; 7:17) and after (9:28; 10:10; 13:3) that event. In short, there is little if any literary evidence to justify the contention that 8:27–30 represents a turning point in Mark's portrayal of the career of Jesus.

Again, this pericope cannot be seen as the center of the Gospel because of the confession of Jesus as Christ. That title does not play a key role in Mark's understanding of Jesus (it plays, as we shall see in the next chapter, a relatively colorless role in Mark's Christology), nor is there a correspondingly positive confession of Jesus as Christ, by Peter or anyone else, to offset the negative overtones of Peter's confession which the subsequent narrative reveals. Peter's confession, wrongly intended by Peter, as Mark makes clear (8:32–33), does set the stage for Jesus to announce for the first time the coming fate of the suffering Son of man. If then the confession has any christological significance it is derived from its correction by a title Mark seems to find more adequate to describe Jesus.

Another kind of solution to the problem of the structure of Mark has been proposed by Willi Marxsen (*Mark the Evangelist*). On the assumption that Mark's geographic scheme does not represent history, Marxsen suggests it represents the theological understanding that provides the key to the Gospel. If Mark is responsible for picturing Jesus' initial activity in Galilee, it must be because Mark understood Jesus' decisive activity to have begun there, and thus it will continue there, after the resurrection. Mark is thus urging his readers to return to the land from which the gospel began, there to await Jesus who will return in the immediate future (Marxsen understands 14:28 and 16:7 to refer to Jesus' parousia, his second coming, not his resurrection). Such an understanding takes into account the difficulties we noted earlier with any attempt to find a sequential geographic itinerary for Jesus from the narrative of the Gospel of Mark, but it is based on a series of assumptions which in some instances are rather speculative. That the geographical notations may have theological significance is not to be denied; that they represent the theological key to understanding Mark's narrative is less convincing.

A different approach to the structure of Mark has been proposed by Rudolph Pesch (*Naherwartungen*), who notes that one characteristic of ancient literature, and a tendency of folk literature of widely varying cultures, is a kind of symmetry in structure. That is, the various segments of a literary work tend to contain the same amount of material (much as is the case with chapters in a modern book, including this one!), and thus tend to be about the same length. To put it another way, the same number of lines will be devoted to the narrative in each section. By counting the lines (a technique called stichometry) one can, if one has some idea of the structure, complete the outline of a work. One can also check one's outline in that way to see if the proposed sections are symmetrical. If the architecture of a literary work can be discerned, we may well have a clue to the way the author understood his material, namely, by the way he divided it. Pesch, on the basis of clues in Mark that could signal changes in the narrative and thus the division between segments (e.g., between 3:6

and 7, or between 8:26 and 27), arrives at the following stichometric outline of Mark, divided into six sections:

I   1:2–3:6, composed of 1:2–34; 1:35–45; 2:1–3:6
II   3:7–6:29, composed of 3:7–4:34; 4:35–5:20; 5:21–6:29
III   6:30–8:26, composed of 6:30–7:13; 7:14–23; 7:24–8:36
IV   8:27–10:52, composed of 8:27–9:29; 9:30–50; 10:1–52
V   11:1–12:44, composed of 11:1–26; 11:27–12:12; 12:13–44
VI   14:1–16:8, composed of 14:1–52; 14:52–15:5; 15:6–16:8

In each case, as is evident, the major sections can be divided into three smaller segments, a long, short, and long passage, with the number of lines in the two longer passages of each segment roughly equivalent. Further analysis shows that sections I, III, and V are shorter than II, IV, and VI. If one combines the shorter and longer sections into three larger divisions, one arrives at the following structure:

1:2–6:29, composed of 1:2–3:35; 4:1–12; 4:13–6:29
6:30–10:52, composed of 6:30–8:26; 8:27–9:13; 9:14–10:52
11:1–16:8, composed of 11:1–12:44 and 14:1–11; 14:12–25;
    14:26–16:8

Again, each larger division contains within itself a longer, shorter, and longer passage, with the longer passages in each division roughly the same length. On this arrangement, the "middle" passage would be 8:27–9:13. Finally, taking that as a clue, Pesch suggests that the entire Gospel of Mark can be divided into three parts, a longer, shorter, and longer passage:

1:2–8:26; 8:27–30; 8:31–16:8

The number of lines here would be: 708, 10, 708. Thus the stichometric division of Mark indicates, on this measuring, that the center of the Gospel architectonically is also the middle that others have found using entirely different methods.

This is a most interesting attempt, and careful attention to the divisions he suggests will show that in virtually all instances, the points at which he breaks segments, or sections, or divisions conform to the sense of the narrative. The difficulty, as most readers will already have observed, is the fact that in all these calculations, chap.

13 has had to be omitted. If chap. 13 is included, there is no way that Pesch's pattern can be preserved. That means one of two things: either the pattern is artificial, or Mark added chap. 13 after he had planned and written the remaining fifteen chapters (the latter is Pesch's thesis). To be sure, chap. 13 is a different kind of material from that contained in most of the rest of the Gospel, and it may represent, as some scholars have suggested, an apocalyptic "broadside" which Mark incorporated into his narrative, perhaps even after it was finished. Yet, we have in fact no example of Mark from which chap. 13 has been omitted (an unimportant point if Mark himself added the chapter before releasing his Gospel to the public; more important if a later editor is thought to have added it). More importantly, much of the material in chap. 13 is anticipated in the preceding portions of Mark's narrative, as we shall see later on, and several contemporary scholars have found in chap. 13 the key to unraveling a number of mysteries concerning Mark. The omission of chap. 13 from the original plan of Mark thus remains speculative, and any outline which is forced to omit it must also, therefore, remain speculative.

A satisfactory solution to the problem of the outline of Mark thus remains to be found. Perhaps this is due to insufficient attention to the narrative of Mark on the part of scholars, or perhaps it is due to the fact that Mark himself did not shape his Gospel with any such central point in mind, but rather moved, section by section, to the chronological as well as theological climax of his Gospel. Further attention to the various theological motifs and problems in Mark may help us catch a glimpse of the answer, and it is to those motifs and problems that we must now turn our attention.

CHAPTER FIVE

THE CHRISTOLOGY OF MARK

If the central figure of Mark's Gospel is Jesus of Nazareth, it is equally true that that central figure represents the central problem of this Gospel. Jesus announces things people have been waiting centuries to hear ("The kingdom of God is at hand"; 1:15); he does things that are utterly astonishing ("Who then is this, that even wind and sea obey him?" 4:41); he says things that put a severe strain on the presuppositions and beliefs that made up the normal mental furniture of those who were his closest followers ("And the disciples were amazed at his words," 10:24). It would be quite accurate to say that to solve the problem of Jesus would be to solve the problem of the Gospel of Mark. Scholars have as yet reached no agreement that the problem of Mark has been solved, but a good deal of recent research approaching Mark from a wide variety of perspectives has pointed unmistakably to the fact that a major reason—if not *the* major reason —for the writing of Mark centers around this christological problem. For whatever reasons—because Mark wants to correct some kind of erroneous Christology, or because some historical crisis has called into question earlier christological convictions—the earliest Gospel has among its central problems the question of the correct understanding of Jesus.

An indication of the great importance of the christological question for Mark can be seen at the very outset, in the way in which the preaching of John the Baptist is dealt with in the three synoptic Gospels. In Mark John's very first words concern the one who comes (1:7–8); Jesus is clearly for Mark the focus of all that John had to say. In Matthew, John's first words concern the coming of the kingdom of Heaven, and only after prolonged discussion does John announce the coming of a mightier one (3:2–12). In a similar way in

Luke John is presented debating with Jews and giving advice on how to act in view of the impending wrath of God, before he announces the coming of his greater successor (3:1–17). Clearly, for Mark the ensuing narrative will have as its central concern this Jesus.

Mark used several titles in his narrative to identify Jesus, and we can learn a great deal about how Mark understood Jesus by a careful examination of these titles. Perhaps the most common title, both for us as well as for the contemporaries of Jesus, is "Christ" which simply means "anointed one." Kings and priests were regularly anointed in OT times as a sign of their special relationship to God. It is therefore little wonder that expectations of the coming deliverer were also, because of his God-given mission, understood in terms of one who would be anointed for his task. Thus, "the anointed one" (Hebrew: Messiah; Greek: Christ) came to be a designation in Jewish circles for the one who would come to deliver the Jews from their oppressors. Already by the time Mark began to write, this title had attached itself so closely to Jesus that it virtually formed part of his name. The opening sentence of the narrative identifies the central figure as "Jesus *Christ*." That identification was already common much earlier in the time of Paul, as his letters make clear (e.g., Rom. 1:1). There can thus be little doubt that this title was already common and familiar both to Mark and to his readers when Mark began to write his account of Jesus. Perhaps for that reason, Mark does not invest it with any particular significance in his narrative. Surely it is important. When Peter wants to sum up what Jesus' followers feel about him, it is only natural for Mark to record the tradition that had Peter confess Jesus as "the Christ." Peter's subsequent rebuke is not for using the title, but for trying to keep Jesus from his God-given fate of suffering (8:27–33). When the high priest wanted to find out the extent of the importance Jesus assigned to himself, he naturally phrased the question to include that title: "Are you the Christ?" (14:61). It also comes naturally to Mark as a designation for Jesus in quite neutral circumstances, as in 9:41, where it is used in reference to those who follow Jesus; or in 13:21–22 where Jesus speaks of false "Christs" who will lead people astray because they claim to be the returned Jesus. Mark saw no problem in allowing that title to stand in the traditions as he found them. That the title was problematic, even before Mark, is indicated by an episode which Mark has placed in the temple as one of a series of stories reporting conflicts between Jesus and representatives of various Jewish religious parties. In that episode, Jesus challenges the Jewish assumption that the anointed one is to be a descendant of David (12:35–37). Whether the point of this story is to allow Jesus to claim to be the Christ even though he is not of the Davidic line (Matthew and Luke make it a point to include information that he is, but Mark contains no such traditions about Jesus' ancestry), or to dispute the appropriateness of Jewish messianic expectation (the anointed one cannot be Davidic), Mark can simply allow the title "Christ" to stand as a normal designation of the awaited deliverer.

If the title has no necessary negative connotations in Mark, neither can he use it in any positive solution to the christological problem he faces, if for no other reason than that the title is ambiguous. While in Christian confession it can refer to the Jesus who suffered on the cross, it could also be used to designate a royal deliverer, as is clear when, at the crucifixion, the chief priests and scribes identify the title "Christ" with the title "King of Israel" (15:32). It is clear in Mark that it was as such a royal pretender that Jesus was executed by the Romans, as a glance at the account of the trial before Pilate will show (15:2, 9, 12, 18), and as the official designation of his crime as posted on the cross confirms (15:26). In that light, Mark may intend us to understand that that is what the high priest intended by his question to Jesus: "Are you the Christ?"

There is, however, no hint in Mark, despite the political overtones the title "Christ" carried in some circles, that Mark felt the title inadequate for that reason. Markan scholars used to make much of the conjecture that it was the political implications of the title "Christ" that caused Jesus to reject it when Peter used it, but Mark himself gives no hint that that is the case. The rebuke to Peter (8:33) is a counterpoint to Jesus' prediction of his suffering; that Peter had political yearnings when he used the title is purely an inference based on a guess at Peter's inner psychological processes. Such guesses have rightly been abandoned in modern gospel scholarship.

For whatever reason, then, whether the title "Christ" was too common, too ambiguous, or too filled with possible negative implications, Mark did not feel it was an appropriate one for the particular christological points he wanted to score. Where it appeared in his traditions, he allowed it to stand, but he did not use it to express his own convictions about Jesus.

A second christological title which Mark found in his traditions is "Son of God." This was a title that clearly had a good deal of importance for Mark, because the climactic confession of Jesus in the crucifixion scene makes use of this very title (15:39). We saw in the preceding chapter that traditions which identified Jesus by means of this same title were placed by Mark at the beginning and the approximate midpoint in his narrative (baptism: 1:10–11; transfiguration: 9:2–8). While we saw that these traditions were inadequate to serve as the chief structural elements in the Gospel, their placement clearly indicates that Mark saw them as important. Many early manuscripts also add the title "Son of God" to the end of the first verse in Mark; if they represent the original reading of that verse, then Mark clearly saw this as a very important title.

The problem with this title, as with the title "Christ," lies in its ambiguity. It can carry a high degree of significance, but it also could be used in a quite neutral way, as its use at 13:32 shows. In that passage, it simply differentiates the Son from the Father, although in a way that shows the limitations of the Son compared to the Father. Even more, however, the title was at least as ambiguous as the title "Christ," as its employment by the demons clearly shows (3:11; 5:7). In one of those instances (3:11), an editorial summary written by Mark, Jesus would not allow the demons to use that title, perhaps indicating the ambiguity inherent in it. The use of a form of this title, "Son of the Blessed," ("Blessed" was a Jewish circumlocution for God) by the high priest during Jesus' trial, especially in association with the term "Christ," simply confirms the ambiguous nature of this title. What the high priest meant by that designation, and what the confession of the centurion conveys in Mark's narrative, are worlds apart.

There are some other designations for Jesus that carry christological implications that we may assume Mark found inadequate, since he did not give them a central role in his narrative. "Son of David," which as we saw, was contested in a controversy story, was also applied to Jesus by the blind Bartimaeus (10:47, 48). There is a strong later Jewish tradition which saw in Solomon, David's son and successor on the throne of Israel, the originator of the magical arts, and as a result many of the magical traditions which filled the Hellenistic world to overflowing were assigned to him. There is, of course, no way of knowing whether such an identification of Solomon as master of the magical arts is implied when a blind man seeking help addresses Jesus as "Son of David." For whatever reason, however, this title was not a popular one in the pre-Markan traditions, nor did Mark place any weight on it in his narrative. Another such designation for Jesus is "prophet." Jesus seems, by implication at least, to attribute this title to himself in the account of his rejection at Nazareth (6:4), but it is clearly not a satisfactory title for that purpose, so far as Mark is concerned. Its further use is restricted to traditions that report the popular image of Jesus among the masses: they see him as a prophet, or as Elijah returned (6:15; 8:28).

There is one title, however, that Mark found eminently suited to his purposes. That title is "Son of man." There is at present no scholarly consensus concerning the importance of this title in pre-Christian Jewish traditions. The phrase can, of course, mean simply man in a generic sense, as it does in Ps. 8:4, where it stands in parallelism to "man." In the pre-Markan tradition that may have been the meaning of Mark 2:28. There "man" and "Son of man" stand in similar parallelism. That couplet, added by Mark to the story of Jesus and his disciples passing through a grain field on the sabbath, may originally have been a saying of Jesus giving "man" simply as a human being authority over the sabbath, thus freeing him from the innumerable restrictions rabbinic legal exegesis had placed upon his sabbath behavior. In its present context in Mark, of course, there can be no doubt that the "Son of man" who is Lord of the sabbath is Jesus.

This title also occurs in Jewish traditions where it is used to designate a figure more than just human. In Dan. 7:13, the phrase, highly qualified, is used to describe the central figure in Daniel's fifth nightvision who ultimately receives dominion over all the peoples of the earth. This figure is interpreted as the "saints of the Most High" in v. 18, thus making it represent the faithful remnant of Israel. The title also occurs in later apocryphal writings. In 1 Enoch it designates a figure who in the last times will judge and overthrow the wicked and uphold the righteous (chaps. 46–53), and he is also called the "Anointed one" and the "Elect one," thus clearly designating him an eschatological deliverer of Israel. In 4 Ezra a similar eschatological avenger is described, but his title is simply "Man," although it may belong to the "Son of man" tradition.

The extent to which this title represented a firm set of eschatological expectations in the time of Jesus has been much debated, as has the question whether or not an actual figure designated with the title "Son of man" was expected to appear in the last times. It is very difficult, therefore, to come to any firm conclusion about what expectations the Jews of Jesus' time associated with this title, if indeed it was a familiar eschatological title to them at all. In one passage in Mark which Mark appears to have assembled from his traditions, Jesus seems to be referring to the Son of man as someone different from himself (8:38). If, however, Jesus ever did speak of a Son of man as someone different from himself, by the time Mark wrote his Gospel, that title had been firmly attached to Jesus.

Whatever conclusion we may want to reach on the pre-Christian expectations attached to the title "Son of man," it is clear that Mark feels this title is the one most adequate to express the meaning of Jesus of Nazareth. It can be used to designate Jesus during his earthly career. At the very beginning of his account of Jesus' activity, Mark places two traditions in which that title refers to Jesus as he carried on his ministry in Galilee (2:1–12; 2:27–28). The title can also be used to refer to Jesus as the one who was betrayed (14:21), arrested (14:41), who suffered (9:12) and died (10:45), who was raised from the dead (9:9), who was seated at God's right hand in heaven (14:26), and who would come at the end of the age to gather the faithful into God's kingdom (13:26).

It is obvious that Mark can use this designation to correct the more familiar christological titles that also appeared in the traditions he had at his disposal, but which were open to ambiguous understanding. When Peter confesses that Jesus is the Christ, Jesus responds with a statement of the impending fate of the Son of man, thus implicitly correcting the former title by the latter one (8:29–31). The same holds true of the trial scene. There, when the high priest combines the two familiar christological titles in his question to Jesus, Jesus acknowledges the applicability of those titles to himself, but then corrects them by referring to himself as the Son of man (14:61–62). A further indication of the importance of this title for

Mark's christological understanding of Jesus lies in the fact that Jesus is the only one in the whole of the Gospel who uses this title. Mark presents this one christological designation as the favorite title of Jesus for himself. Not only does this make clear its unambiguous nature, so far as Mark is concerned, but it also, again so far as Mark is concerned, was capable of expressing Jesus' own self-understanding. This self-understanding, implied in most of the passages where the title Son of man is used, is perhaps best expressed when Jesus speaks of himself as one who serves, and who will die for others (10:45).

It is in fact this understanding of Jesus as one who must suffer, die, and who will rise, that represents the controlling christological emphasis in Mark's Gospel. If Jesus is the key to the Gospel narrative, then Jesus as suffering Son of man gives us the clue to unravel many of the mysteries that present themselves to the reader of that narrative. We will see in the pages that follow how the concept of Jesus' suffering clarifies again and again the intention of passages that otherwise are obscure and enigmatic.

If there is, for example, a characteristic difference between the first and second halves of the Gospel, it lies precisely in the fact that once Jesus' suffering is announced (8:31), it dominates the narrative from that point on. It is the clue to the relationship between the careers of John the Baptist and Jesus (9:12), something already implied in the account of the death of John (6:14–29). It is, furthermore, the clue to understanding the nature of discipleship. In each of the three instances in chaps. 8–10, where Mark has placed words of Jesus that speak of discipleship, those words are introduced with a prediction that Jesus will have to suffer (8:31; 9:31; 10:33–34). Each of those predictions, in turn, has been shaped in its vocabulary by the account Mark gives of the suffering and death of Jesus in the concluding portion of the Gospel. Furthermore, as has often been noted, the events of the final week of Jesus' life occupy a far larger proportion of Mark's narrative about Jesus' public career than they did in that public career itself. The final seven days in Jerusalem constitute the subject matter of more than one-third of the Gospel. That in itself is a clear indication of where Mark locates the importance of the story of Jesus.

Here again, however, one cannot draw absolute conclusions about differences between the two halves of Mark's Gospel. If the emphasis on Jesus' suffering becomes apparent after 8:31, the reader is not unprepared for such a fate for Jesus. Jesus' disputes with the religious leaders begin early in Mark's account (2:1), and the reader is left with little doubt that the outcome of those disputes will be lethal for Jesus (3:6). The attentive reader will realize from that point on the likely outcome of the growing opposition to Jesus, and will be reminded of that impending fate each time another dispute with such leaders is reported. John the Baptist, with whose appearance Mark tells us the gospel of Jesus begins, suffers violent death (6:27–28), and if we do not associate that with Jesus' fate immediately, we are later informed that that is its meaning (9:12). How else, finally, are we to understand the first announcement that Jesus' journey will end in Jerusalem, with its strange information that the mere act of Jesus walking down the road to Jerusalem inspires fear and amazement in those who accompany him, than to understand it as further indication of the suffering that awaits him at the climax of his earthly life? From end to end (the last christological title, God's Son, prompted by the sight of Jesus' death, is also the first, at the baptism—does Mark think of Jesus as baptised into his career as one who suffers?), Mark's Gospel is pervaded by the understanding that Jesus cannot be understood unless he is recognized as the one who must suffer.

Yet not only as one who suffers; again and again, the announcement of suffering is coupled with the announcement that Jesus will subsequently rise from the dead (8:31; 9:9; 9:31; 10:34; in addition, his rising is presumed in 8:38; 13:26; 14:62, and probably also in 14:25). The question of whether or not these traditions accurately reflect the thought of the historical Jesus is not at issue. The point is, included as they are in Mark's narrative, they do show Mark's understanding of Jesus, and indicate where he sees Jesus' importance to lie. Mark's Gospel centers in Jesus, and he presents that Jesus as one who moves forward to his destiny on the cross, subsequently to rise as victor from the grave. The absence of resurrection appearances at the conclusion of the Gospel may be strange to us who know the later Gospels, but there can be no question that Mark knew that death was unable to hold Jesus, and that he had been vindicated from his criminal's death when he left the grave.

If this is Mark's understanding of the meaning of Jesus, it may also help to clarify his use of the word "gospel" itself. That particular problem is confronted as soon as one begins to read Mark's narrative; it begins with the strange statement that it begins (1:1)! That first verse has long been regarded as puzzling. It is hardly a superscription. No reader needs to be told a book begins at the beginning. Some have argued it means that the gospel of Jesus begins with the appearance of John the Baptist, but the language is such that the sentence about John begins with v. 2. The problem would be solved if by "gospel" Mark meant something other than simply the narrative that follows, or something other than a kind of literature, or a book. The word has come to mean that, but could Mark have meant something different?

An examination of the way Mark uses the word "gospel" throws a good deal of light on that problem. So unique is his use of this word that he may have been the one who introduced it into the traditions about Jesus. It is interesting to note that Mark is the only Gospel in which the word "gospel" is used in an absolute sense. Matthew employs the word only four times, in every case with a qualifying word attached (4:23; 9:35; 24:14; 26:13), and Luke omits it entirely from his Gospel. Luke does use it twice in Acts, but in both instances to designate the content of Paul's missionary preaching (15:7; 20:24). Mark uses the word seven times, four of them in the absolute sense. Equally interesting for an understanding of the way Mark used the word are the passages where the gospel is equated with Jesus himself (". . . whoever loses his life for my sake and for the gospel's," 8:35; ". . . for my sake and for the gospel," 10:29). Apparently, to do something for the "gospel" is to do it for Jesus. In that case, "gospel" must mean something more than a book, or a narrative. Again, after the woman anointed Jesus at Bethany, Jesus says that her deed will be recounted "wherever the gospel is preached in the whole world" (14:9). This means that the gospel includes in itself the story of the career of Jesus, and Mark anticipates that it will receive worldwide proclamation. The same point is made in 13:10: the "gospel" will be preached in all the world. But even more, the gospel is something to be believed (1:15). In fact, the call to believe the gospel is itself part of the preaching of the gospel (1:14–15)! None of this sounds strange to anyone who has read the letters of Paul, but that is just the point: Mark's use of "gospel" is much closer to Paul's use than to that of the other evangelists.

Therefore, the gospel, as Mark uses the word, is more than a book, and more than a narrative or a collection of facts. It is something for which one must be willing to sacrifice one's life, if one is to find that life (8:35). Yet, for the whole of Mark's narrative, as for this verse, the only one through whom we can gain life is Jesus. It would appear, therefore, that the power of Jesus operates through the gospel. Where the gospel is, there Jesus is also present with his power to save. Apparently the narrative of Jesus' deeds and words, accepted as a narrative of deeds done and words spoken by the authority of God is able to save a person's life. Consequently, the unforgivable sin is to attribute Jesus' deeds and words to the devil rather than to God's saving power (3:28–30).

That means that when Mark speaks of the "beginning of the gospel of Jesus Christ," he is not referring to where a book, or even a public career begins, but rather to the fact that God's saving acts, contained in the "gospel," began with the career of Jesus. The implication then is that God's saving acts in Jesus continue in power, a point made explicit in those passages that presume the gospel will continue to be announced and believed after Jesus' earthly career is over (13:10; 14:9). Where the gospel is present, there Jesus' power is present, and perhaps even Jesus himself! In that case, the beginning of the gospel is the career of Jesus which eventuated in his death and resurrection, which in turn makes it possible for the risen Jesus to be present where the good news of his saving words and deeds is announced.

Mark's Christology of the suffering and rising Jesus thus influenced the way he used the word which in the later tradition came to identify the story of the career of Jesus. Unlike Matthew and Luke, Mark understands the gospel to be, not the content of what Jesus says or does, but the power of Jesus himself, present where his story is told. The gospel is the announcement of what God is doing in Jesus, and therefore its beginning was the career of that Jesus. This is simply further confirmation that Mark's Christology of the suffering and risen Jesus informs his entire understanding of the career of Jesus, and it may provide a clue as to why Mark thought a narrative was the only useful means to accomplish the reinterpretation of the Jesus tradition he felt compelled to undertake. We will want to reflect more on that later. First, however, we must consider some of the other aspects of the career of Jesus which Mark narrates.

Kingdom.

CHAPTER SIX

JESUS AS PREACHER

In addition to Mark's presentation of the meaning of Jesus through the device of reporting and reinterpreting certain christological titles, Mark shows Jesus in a variety of activities which also tell us a good deal about the way Mark understood Jesus. We shall deal with three of these activities in the next three chapters, namely, the way in which Mark presents Jesus as preacher, as teacher, and as miracle worker. A careful investigation of the evidence contained in Mark which relates to these three activities will aid us materially in our attempt to get at the intention of Mark's interpretation of the traditions about Jesus, and the way in which Mark understood the earthly career of his risen Lord.

It must be admitted at the outset that the division between Jesus' activities as preacher and those as teacher is somewhat artificial, especially since much of what we would consider "preaching" Mark specifically places under the rubric "teaching" (e.g., the parables). On the other hand, Mark does include in his vocabulary (whether stemming from him or from his traditions) the words for both teaching and preaching, and it may therefore be instructive to examine the differences in his use of those two concepts. Again, since in Mark's narrative Jesus deals with the kingdom of God in material Mark designates as both preaching and teaching, there would be justification to treat that theme under either (or both!) of the discussions relative to those two activities. Because Mark introduced the topic "kingdom of God" in his programmatic statement of Jesus' appearance and activity (1:14–15), which Mark identifies as "preaching," *Kingdom* we will deal with that topic in this chapter. As we shall see, however, the vocabulary identifying Jesus as teacher is even more important to Mark than the vocabulary identifying him as preacher. The signifi-

51

cance of that difference may become clearer in the course of our discussion.

For Mark the fact that Jesus went about preaching was of importance. The first figure we meet in our Gospel is John the Baptist and we hear of him first of all that he was "preaching." This indicates the importance of preaching since for Mark John is the forerunner of Jesus, a forerunner not only in what he says, but also in what happened to him. But John is only a forerunner in Mark. Unlike Matthew, Mark is not willing to allow the content of what John preached to anticipate Jesus' announcement of the coming kingdom (cp. Mark 1:4 with Matt. 3:2). For Mark, the content of John's preaching is repentance, and the announcement that he is merely the forerunner.

Further indication of the importance for Mark's understanding of Jesus as one who went about preaching is to be found in his introduction to Jesus' public ministry. The first thing we learn about his activity is that it included preaching (1:14–15). In fact, the placement of this information may mean to imply that everything Mark wants to tell us subsequently about Jesus is to be understood under the rubric of Jesus' proclamation that the time long awaited was fulfilled, and that with him, the kingdom of God was now dawning. If so, then preaching is the common denominator to which all Jesus' activity can be reduced. Furthermore, since for Mark "gospel" means God's saving activity begun with Jesus' career and continued where that career is announced and accepted as God's act of mercy to sinful man, then the call to "believe in the gospel" which follows the proclamation of the kingdom being at hand takes on added significance as a way to summarize all Mark wants to say about Jesus. All that we hear Jesus say, and all that we see him do, and the wrenching story of his final fate, constitute the content of what it means that Jesus preaches: "the kingdom of God is at hand." Therefore the only appropriate response now for men is to repent (probably understood by Mark in the OT prophetic sense of returning to God) and believe in the gospel.

This insight seems to be confirmed in the next passage in Mark where he used the Greek word for "preaching" (*kērussō*). After a summary which Mark wrote to indicate the extensive nature of Jesus' healing activity (1:32–34), he brings the passage in which Jesus tells his disciples his own understanding of his mission: he must go about the land preaching (1:38). This, says Jesus, is the reason for his existence. That the very next verse (1:39) and the very next story (1:40–45) both tell of healings seems to strengthen the impression that Jesus' total itinerant mission is to be understood as his "preaching."

This might help to explain Mark's subsequent use of the word for "preaching." Mark shows a remarkable reticence in identifying, after 1:14–15, the content of the preaching of Jesus. Jesus does not tell what he must preach in 1:38, nor are we told its content in 1:39. When we are told in 1:45 that preaching made entry into cities impossible, we are given no hint about the content of that preaching. When Jesus chooses twelve to be with him, and to be sent forth to preach (and to cast out demons), we are given no indication about the content of what they were to preach. When they were sent out (6:12) it was with the command to preach "repentance," which is all we learned about the content of Jesus' preaching as well (1:15). At the same time they are to cast out demons and heal the sick.

Perhaps this reticence in spelling out the content of Jesus' preaching is explained by the fact that the content of preaching is to be the gospel itself (cf. 13:10; 14:9, two more places where Mark used the word for "preaching"). The gospel for Mark means the things Jesus did as well as said. Such a conjecture receives at least partial support in the fact that when, on Jesus' command, the healed demoniac from Gerasa returns to his own people to preach, the content of his preaching is "everything Jesus did for him" (5:20). Further support can be derived from the fact that in the story of the deaf-mute (7:32–37), the statement that the people preach (this time contrary to Jesus' command, v. 36) after seeing the healing, implies that what they proclaimed is what they saw, i.e., a healing act of Jesus.

The references in Mark to this point in this chapter exhaust the places Mark used the normal term for "preaching" (kērussō). Nowhere does he use the noun for the content (kērygma) or for the preacher (kēryx; as we shall see, he does not show a similar reticence with the vocabulary for "teaching"). A second word, which means "to announce good news" (euaggelizomai), so important for Luke and for Paul, is absent altogether in Mark. If the specific terminology for "preaching" is limited to those passages, however, the same idea can be expressed in more general language, i.e., in words that mean

simply "speak" (*legō, laleō*), or that mean simply "word" (*logos*).
Thus, the phrase "speak the word" can be used as an exact parallel to
the more specific term "preach" (e.g., 1:15; 1:45; cf. 14:9). But it
can also be used as an exact parallel for the specific term "teach"
(4:33; 8:32; 9:31, where in each instance, the context of Jesus'
speaking has been identified as "teaching"). In fact, *logos* itself, in
the explanation of the parable of the sower (4:14–20), means the
spreading of the Christian message, whether by preaching or teaching.
In most instances, no content is given, not even in the parable's
explanation, where the material concerns exclusively the different ways
the "word" is received, and nothing is said about the content of that
word. If the content is not always specified, however, and if it is not
always clear whether Mark meant the term *logos* to mean "preaching"
or "teaching," it is very clear that Jesus' words are important. One's
final fate will be determined by one's present attitude to Jesus' words
(8:38), and those words themselves have eternal character: heaven
and earth are transitory, but the words of Jesus are eternal (13:31).

What can we conclude from such a survey? Mark did not feel it
necessary either to make consistent use of the words belonging to the
specific vocabulary for "preaching," nor in every instance to exercise
care in assuring that the reader knew the content of the proclamation,
wherever the act was mentioned. Perhaps, as we already suggested,
Mark understood everything Jesus did as "proclamation," and perhaps he understood everything Jesus did as the content of that proclamation. For that reason, to have put more emphasis on the specific
vocabulary, or more restriction on the content, would have accomplished just the opposite of what he intended. All that Jesus does
"preaches," and the content of that preaching therefore must be "all
that Jesus does." Yet we have seen that in that first, programmatic
announcement of Jesus' public ministry, Mark did specify the content
of Jesus' preaching: it was the announcement that the kingdom of
God was now at hand. An examination of this latter phrase, kingdom
of God, may help clarify Mark's intention.

There is no question that for Mark, the appearance of Jesus and
the appearance of the kingdom are closely linked. Jesus' initial announcement in Mark deals with it (1:15), and despite the fact that
such immediate expectation of the kingdom could result in great
mischief, and even had to be countered (cf. 13:6–7, 8b, 10, 21–22,

32, 33), it nevertheless remained Mark's conviction that the kingdom was in fact to be expected in the near if not the immediate future. Jesus says that explicitly in Mark (9:1; 13:30), and on other occasions implied it if he did not say it in so many words (e.g., 14:25). There have been attempts to weaken the force of these statements in Mark, but they remain without real persuasive power. To argue, for example, that 9:1 is fulfilled in the following story of the transfiguration is to bend 9:1 almost completely out of shape. One can hardly argue with much conviction that seeing Jesus transfigured represents the kingdom of God come with power, especially since the events that must happen prior to that coming with power are outlined rather explicitly in chap. 13. The statement in 9:1 that some standing there will not die before that happened implies clearly that some will die, a point left completely out of consideration by those who posit the fulfillment in the next verses. Whatever we may want to make of it, or at whose feet we may want to lay responsibility for this particular formulation (Mark, the primitive community, or Jesus himself), the problem remains that Mark, by including such formulations, intended his reader to understand that the kingdom was imminent, within the lifetime of the generation of Jesus. The fact that we know it did not occur (Mark 13:32–33 was truer than even Mark himself anticipated) ought not blind us to the fact that Mark thought it would. That may add to our burden of interpretation, but we must confront it, if we are to understand what Mark is trying to say. Again, the announcement about the kingdom in that programmatic first statement (1:15) also contains a reference to its nearness. This may imply that in everything that follows the imminence of the kingdom is being demonstrated. Mark apparently wants to tell his readers that the contours of God's coming rule can be seen in the words and events of Jesus of Nazareth. In that case, Jesus and the kingdom would be closely identified.

Furthermore, how one fared in God's kingdom depended on how one ordered one's life now. This can be framed in a very general way, so that one's activities in very broad areas of life are taken into account, as in the series of sayings beginning with 9:43. Although the first two speak of "life" rather than kingdom of God, the noun "life" in Mark always means "eternal life" (cf. also 10:17, 30), and in these particular instances, the presence of the phrase "kingdom of

God" in the third saying (9:47) shows the context within which Mark understood the sayings. Here, clearly, a life of sin, brought on by not sacrificing the member that causes such sin, will keep one from entering the kingdom of God. Whatever one wishes to make of the image of entering maimed in some way into the kingdom of God, the intention of the sayings is clear: what one does now has eternal consequences. A similar intention is probably to be seen in the saying in 10:15, where those who do not receive the kingdom "as a little child" (in meekness? with gratitude? as an unearned gift? unquestioningly?) will not enter it. Again, however one may want to understand childlikeness in this saying, it is clear that one's present activities affect one's future in the kingdom.

There is some indication also that for Mark, entry into the kingdom is dependent on following Jesus. This is surely implied in such a statement as 8:38, where one's fate in judgment is linked to one's acceptance or rejection of Jesus now. Some scholars have argued that the full tradition, of which 8:38 is the negative half, may be found in Luke 12:8–9. In that case, to accept Jesus is to be accepted at the final judgment, and granted entry into the kingdom. To reject him is to insure future rejection. Mark seems to want to make that point as well in the way he has juxtaposed the traditions in 10:17–31. This passage includes the story of a rich man who finds he cannot do what Jesus says he must if he is to gain eternal life (= entering the kingdom); a set of sayings on the difficulty of the rich, indeed of everyone, to enter the kingdom (impossible for men but possible for God, v. 27); and finally a saying on the rewards of following Jesus, even at the cost of sacrificing all things. The point of the last segment (vv. 28–31) is clearly that following Jesus will have its rewards both in this world and in the next, and it may well be that Mark wants us to understand that first story in the same light: to follow Jesus is to enter the kingdom, and when the rich man in the story refuses to follow Jesus, he excludes himself from the kingdom. This same point seems to be implied in Mark's story of the scribe who asks Jesus about the most important command in the law (12:28–34). This scribe, of all those who questioned Jesus in this section of Mark's narrative (12:1–44), is the only one who reacts favorably to Jesus (v. 32), and Jesus tells him he is "not far from the kingdom of God" (v. 34). It may well be that again Mark understands this in the sense that following Jesus means entry into the kingdom, and that such agreement with Jesus is the first step in following him. Similarly, the identification of Joseph of Arimethea, who showed his respect for Jesus by burying his body, as one who was "looking for the kingdom of God" (15:43) may well imply that the two items are related: his expectation of the kingdom may stem, at least in Mark's understanding, from the obvious honor in which he held Jesus.

A final indication of the relationship between one's attitude to Jesus and one's fate in God's kingdom may well be found in the fact that the only unforgivable sin Mark reports involves one's estimate of Jesus. To deny he works by God's power (in this pericope, 3:28–30, the context is the Pharisees' identification of Jesus' power with that of Satan, v. 22) is to set oneself under the burden of an unforgivable sin, and surely, in Mark's understanding that means one is excluded from entry into God's kingdom.

We should note that Mark never really tells us much about this kingdom other than some indication of who may enter it. Perhaps this is due to the fact that Mark could suppose his readers knew all about the Jewish traditions concerning God's final, righteous rule, when his Lordship, proclaimed by OT prophets, would become visible, and everyone would know he was the one who ruled the entire creation. Yet surely Jewish readers would not need the kind of information Mark provides in 7:3–4, or the translation of Aramaic phrases which Mark provides in 5:41; 7:34 and 15:22, 34. What, in Mark's view, is this kingdom of God?

The only explicit statement Mark makes about the kingdom in that vein is—the kingdom is a mystery! That statement itself is so "mysterious" that both Matthew and Luke thought they had to clear it up, so both changed Mark 4:11 to read: "to you (i.e., the disciples) has been given *to know* the mysteries of the kingdom of God" (Matt. 13:11; Luke 8:10). Both Matthew and Luke thus thought the statement had to do with information of some sort which the disciples understood but others did not. That is not what Mark appears to want to say, however. He does not attribute the disciples' favored position to something they know. Mark makes this statement in full awareness of the picture he intends to draw of the disciples as men who were incapable, during Jesus' ministry, of understanding him or what he was talking about (e.g., 6:52; 7:18; 8:17; 9:32, to mention but a few instances). Their having the mystery of the kingdom is thus unlikely in Mark to mean they had comprehended some secret information. Whatever the mystery of the kingdom may be for Mark, it cannot rest on something one clearly understands, or at least that the disciples clearly understood. That point is reinforced in one of the parables Jesus tells (4:26–29). If the harvest continues to bear the figurative meaning it had in some OT traditions, then this parable has something to do with God's final judgment, since the figures of harvest and reaping were figures of that last event (this has carried over in other NT writings as well; cf. Matt. 3:12; 13:36–43). It is also clear that the seed that is planted and grows plays a key part in the parable, yet that is precisely the event that is identified in the parable itself as a mystery: the farmer who plants the seed and awaits the harvest does not know how the seed grows (4:27)! In fact, he goes about his ordinary business, unaware of how the key event happens. We will have more to say in the next chapter about how Mark understood parables, but at this point in our discussion it is sufficient to note the mystery at the heart of a parable precisely about the kingdom of God! That the smallest seed should produce the largest garden shrub (4:30–32) also has something of the mysterious about it.

What is this mystery which those who follow Jesus have been given, and those who do not follow him do not have? If it is not some kind of information, what did Mark think it was? There has been, and continues to be, so much disagreement among scholars on this question that any answer must be guarded. Yet, in the light of everything else we have seen about the way Mark understood the kingdom of God, would it not have to include in its meaning the fact that the difference between the two groups is that the disciples follow Jesus? Must it not include in its meaning the fact that the disciples, the twelve and the others who follow him (both groups are explicitly mentioned in this very context, 4:10), have seen in Jesus something important enough to have given up all else to follow (cp. 8:34–37 with 10:28)? The mystery given to them is—fellowship with Jesus. They do not understand him or all that he says, yet they continue to follow him about Galilee. They do not let their puzzlement or their inability to understand what he says deter them from listening to what he says, and following him wherever he goes.

That does not solve the problem entirely, however, for in the end, the disciples do not follow him. At the last, crucial moment, when they are called upon to fulfill the final demand of discipleship (cf. 8:34–35), they desert Jesus and flee (14:50). And surely it is not accidental that the disciple who has the most to say in Mark's Gospel about his resolve to follow Jesus no matter what (14:29–31) is the one whose denial is told in most detail (14:66–72). He, as they, broke fellowship with Jesus in the final, critical moment.

Yet Mark knew of that tradition, too, as he wrote 4:11. Thus the mystery remains a mystery to the end. Do the disciples finally come to the point that they do understand clearly, and follow faithfully, this Jesus who is wrapped about with the mystery of God's final design for human kind? Is the mystery ever revealed, or does it end with the final dying cry of Jesus from the cross? To ask the question is to hint at the answer, but we must look more carefully at some other aspects of the way Mark pictured Jesus before we will be in a position to undertake an answer.

CHAPTER SEVEN

JESUS AS TEACHER

Teacher

There is compelling evidence that Mark saw in Jesus' activity as teacher the central thrust of his mission as the one who announced the inbreaking of God's rule. Again and again, in summaries he has composed, he identifies Jesus as teacher, or names his activity "teaching." Again and again, he has Jesus addressed as "teacher," frequently in contexts so strange that the two evangelists who later incorporated much of his material into their own narratives about Jesus either changed or omitted such an address. The range of material Mark presents under the rubric "teaching" is varied in content, audience, and method, and while he can give examples of what the content of that teaching was, he can also simply designate Jesus' activity as "teaching," and let it go at that. Far more often than Mark tells us that Jesus preached, he specifically tells us that Jesus functioned as teacher. However we may want to account for that fact, the evidence is there, and it is persuasive. The changes Matthew and Luke make in the Markan picture of Jesus do not place such an emphasis on Jesus as teacher but rather lessen it. They may have drawn from their other sources more examples of the sayings of Jesus, but it would be quite wrong to say that the main point on which they wished to correct Mark was to identify Jesus as teacher (as against, e.g., a miracle worker). It would be difficult to put more emphasis on Jesus as teacher than Mark does. It is most instructive for our understanding of Mark's interpretation of the Jesus tradition to examine the way in which he presents Jesus as teacher.

While it is easy to be misled by word-use statistics, in this case they do give an accurate picture of the relationship between Mark on the one hand and Luke and Matthew on the other so far as their views of Jesus as teacher are concerned. All three employ the words for this activity ("teacher," "teaching" as noun and verb) in about the same quantity, which of course means that since Mark has only about three-fifths of the volume of Matthew or Luke, he uses the vocabulary with considerably more frequency. Even more interesting is the fact that of the 31 instances where Mark uses one of the three words meaning specifically "teacher" or "teaching," there are only five of those which both Matthew and Luke have decided to reproduce, and in twenty of those cases, neither Matthew nor Luke chose to reproduce it. Either they drop the material, or substitute other vocabulary. Whatever else that may mean, it tends to indicate that Mark used this kind of language in a way that, in a majority of cases, neither Matthew nor Luke felt was particularly appropriate. A detailed consideration of each of these instances would require more space than this small book will allow, yet its undertaking, simple enough with a concordance, will yield significant results for one's understanding of the theological stance of each of the three synoptic authors.

What then can we say of the way Mark understood Jesus as teacher? Clearly, Mark thought of it as a characteristic activity of Jesus. Time and again, Mark includes in his narrative stories in which Jesus functions the way a teacher of the law, a rabbi, would have functioned in that time and place. A man asks him: "Teacher, what must I do to inherit eternal life?" (10:17), and Jesus answers out of the law. Pharisees, Herodians, and Sadducees, bent on trapping him by what he says, address him as "teacher," and engage him in the kind of discussions about the Jewish law they found quite normal (12:14, 19). A scribe, hearing his answer about the most important command in that law, acknowledges him as "teacher" (12:32).

Jesus' disciples also use that designation in addressing him, and use it in situations that have nothing to do with such activity on his part (9:38; 10:35; 13:1). Mark reports that Jesus taught in synagogues (1:21; 6:2), the normal place for such activity, but also, in summary statements that Mark himself composed, he reports that Jesus taught beside the sea, where crowds assembled and pressed around him (2:13; 4:1–2; 10:1). In fact, Mark assures us that wherever such crowds gathered, it was Jesus' custom to teach them (10:1). Finally, Jesus himself identifies his daily activity in the temple during the days prior to his arrest as "teaching" (14:49), and designates "teacher" as the title by which he wants his disciples to identify him to a man in a village (14:14).

In his use both of tradition and of composition, therefore, Mark intends to convey to his readers the fact that Jesus functioned as teacher during his earthly career. Perhaps more characteristically, however, than such conventional ways of telling about Jesus as teacher, Mark identifies Jesus as teacher where one would not have expected it. For example, Mark regularly uses the title, or the verb, in connection with miracles of Jesus (1:21–22; 4:38; 5:35; 6:34; 9:17; 9:38; 11:21). In a number of such instances, modern translators find the title as inappropriate in such circumstances as did Matthew and Luke, and so they change it. When the disciples fear for their lives on the stormy sea and plead with Jesus to save them, they address him as "teacher"; Matthew and Luke changed that address, as did the RSV, to "master." The RSV follows the same practice where Mark used the Hebrew-Aramaic designation for teacher, namely "rabbi"; in each case, it is translated as "master," a permissible translation which nevertheless obscures the force of the original (9:5; 10:51; 11:21; 14:45). Again, Jesus in the wilderness with his disciples, seeing the masses milling about, had compassion on them, and Mark tells us his compassion found expression in teaching them. Neither Matthew nor Luke found this an adequate formulation, and both changed it, omitting the specific reference to teaching. Again, when the disciple John wants to complain about a free-lance exorcist who, though not a follower of Jesus, nevertheless is using Jesus' name to achieve results, he addresses Jesus as "teacher," something Luke changed and Matthew omitted altogether (Mark 9:38). We will need to return to the investigation of the relationship Mark saw between Jesus as teacher and as miracle worker later on.

There are other ways in which Mark's preoccupation with Jesus as teacher finds expression in the manner in which he shapes his narrative. For example, when the disciples return from their mission on which Jesus had sent them, they report all that "they had done and taught" (6:30), even though "teaching" was not part of what they had been told to do (cf. 6:7, 12, 13). Mark apparently saw this as such a regular part of Jesus' activity, and so important that even though his tradition did not include it, the reader is told that part of what the disciples had done was to teach. Could the followers of one who so regularly taught crowds in synagogue and at the seashore possibly carry out their assigned mission without also teaching?

Clearly Mark thought not. Again, although Jesus experienced rejection in his homeland so that those who heard his teaching were offended at him and refused all faith in him, to the extent that the normal miraculous activity that accompanied Jesus' teaching and preaching was significantly reduced (6:4–6a), this did not have any effect on Jesus' continued activity as teacher. If he did not perform his customary healings because of their lack of faith, it did not hinder his teaching: "And he went about among the villages teaching," Mark tells us.

In such varied ways we can see that Mark, when he shaped the traditions at his disposal into the narrative of Jesus, took from the tradition, and introduced, references to Jesus as teacher where that was most appropriate. He also included such references where they were not so appropriate, at least not in the view of those who were otherwise so impressed with his narrative as a whole that they modeled theirs after it, namely Matthew and Luke. There is yet more to learn about Mark's understanding of the meaning of Jesus as teacher than can be gleaned from such a general survey of some of the evidence. That meaning for Mark is, it would appear, inextricably bound with Mark's understanding of Jesus as miracle worker.

The place to begin an investigation of that understanding is with the first miracle story Mark records (1:21–27). Even a quick reading shows that the framework of the story concerns Jesus as teacher, while the story itself is a healing miracle in the form of the expulsion of a demon. Furthermore, the high incidence of Markan vocabulary and grammatical structure points to Mark as the one who is responsible for giving to this story the framework it now has in his Gospel. We have again, therefore, on a smaller scale, a use of traditions similar to the use we found in the account of the cleansing of the temple: a story is bracketed by traditions that interpret it. The interpretation here, indicated both by the juxtaposition as well as the content of the introduction and conclusion provided by Mark, clearly intends to point to the power of Jesus' teaching. Not only does Mark *tell* us that Jesus' teaching in the synagogue elicited astonishment from those who heard it because of its power and authority (vv. 22, 27), he also provides us with an *example* of the power and authority Jesus possessed: a power that let him simply speak a word, and a demon, a servant of Satan (3:22 indicates that was the way demons were understood, had no choice but to obey. The implication is clear: Jesus' power that permits him such incredible acts of authority is also present in his spoken word when he teaches. Even the very command by which the act of power against the demon is carried out is identified as "teaching" (v. 27). Could Mark more clearly indicate the importance of Jesus as teacher than by such a demonstration of the power inherent in his words? Interestingly enough, both Matthew and Luke apparently thought there were other ways to show what it meant that Jesus was a teacher, and both changed this story from Mark in such a way that the emphasis was no longer on Jesus' teaching. Matthew omitted the miracle altogether, and used the verse about astonishment at Jesus' teaching as the reaction to the Sermon on the Mount (7:28-29). Thus Matthew chose a different way—a long teaching session of Jesus (cf. 5:2)—to show the authority with which Jesus taught. Luke keeps the introduction (Luke 4:31-32), but alters the conclusion so the reaction now concerns just the miracle, not the teaching (4:36). That is a rather clear indication that this story in Mark represents Mark's own understanding, one which the other two evangelists found either strange or inappropriate, and so they changed it.

Mark, of course, can also point to the astonishment of people at Jesus' teaching in contexts other than miracle stories (e.g., 6:2; 11:18), but this initial episode surely indicates that for Mark the power of Jesus' words which caused such astonishment was the same power as that which was narrated in that first story. Jesus' power is as apparent in his teaching as in his exorcisms. That may also explain Mark's desire to have Jesus addressed as "teacher" in the midst of miracle stories, where, as the changes of Matthew and Luke again show, we are dealing with a uniquely Markan understanding of Jesus and the power of his teaching. The request to save the disciples from the stormy sea is preceded by the address "teacher" (4:38). The messenger from the household of Jairus, come to tell Jairus that his daughter is dead and beyond the power of a healer, identifies Jesus as "teacher" (5:35). The father of a possessed boy, having brought his child in search of Jesus and healing, precedes his request for help by addressing Jesus as "teacher" (9:17). The Aramaic form of that address (rabbi) is used by the blind Bartimaeus when he asks for healing (10:51), and by Peter as he calls attention to the fact that the fig tree which Jesus had cursed had withered (11:21). Such evidence indicates that the identification of the wondrous power of Jesus' teaching, established with the first miracle story in the Gospel, is continued by Mark right through the narrative.

In light of such an understanding of Jesus as teacher, it is surprising that we are not given more specific instances of the content of that teaching. Time and again, we are told Jesus taught without any indication of what it was he said (2:13; 6:2, 6, 34; 10:1). When the content is given, it can be quite short and specific: two of his three announcements of Jesus' impending sufferings are identified by Mark as "teaching" (8:31; 9:31). Jesus' explanation of the reason for his "cleansing" acts within the temple is similarly identified as "teaching" (11:17), as is his discussion about whether or not it can be legitimate to think of the Messiah as David's son (12:35). Mark wanted to show that he was merely giving selections from Jesus' teachings (the phrasing of 4:2 and 12:38 make that clear), but only in one instance are we given the content of a longer teaching session of Jesus. That session is contained in the fourth chapter of Mark's Gospel, to which we must now turn our attention. *ch 4*

The fourth chapter, with its parables and sayings, is the result of Mark's work as editor and assembler of traditions. Mark knew that this was not the only time Jesus spoke in parables (cf. 3:23), but he concentrated the parables he had into this section of his Gospel with the result that we would probably be correct in thinking that Mark understood parables as an important teaching technique of Jesus (cf. 4:33). We would probably also be correct in thinking that what is contained in the parables is an indication of the content of Jesus' teaching as Mark understood that content. Let us consider the evidence that allows us to conclude that Mark assembled this material, and then turn to the content of the material itself.

The theme and vocabulary of 4:1–2 give every indication that Mark composed them. Grammatical constructions that regularly occur in materials for which he seems responsible also occur here, and the themes of "teaching," "sea," and "crowds" are characteristic of Markan summaries. Even the boat Jesus entered seems to presume the present context: Jesus had asked that it be readied in 3:9, but it was not used at that time. Thus grammar, vocabulary, and context all point to the Markan composition of 4:1–2. Furthermore, the parable itself is introduced with a doubled command to pay attention (English translations of 4:3 regularly reproduce only one): "Listen, behold." The parable also has at its conclusion a command to give close heed (v. 9), and that command is introduced by a shortened form of the Markan attachment formula (*kai elegen autois*, here shortened to *kai elegen*; a third variation of the formula is *kai legei autois*). Since the Markan attachment formula also occurs in 4:2, Mark's compositional technique emerges. To a parable that already began with a command to give close heed ("behold," *idou*), Mark provided a framework making the same point ("listen," *akouete*, v. 3; "who has ears to hear, let him hear," v. 9), and put the whole after his introduction to this teaching session of Jesus. V. 10 is also a regular Markan motif (Jesus explains privately to his disciples), and vv. 11–12 are again introduced with the Markan attachment formula. Mark has thus apparently attached this saying about the mystery of the kingdom to this context of a teaching session as well; its significance in this context will become apparent later. The explanation of the parable is again introduced with one of the variations of the Markan attachment formula (v. 13). Perhaps Mark interposed vv. 10–12 between parable and explanation. If he did, then we will have to expect that they interpret each other as has been the case in other places where Mark inserts one tradition into another. The conclusion of the explanation is followed by another attachment formula (v. 21) and two sayings (vv. 22–23). Both Matthew and Luke put those sayings into other contexts, an indication that they circulated independently of the context into which Mark put them. We then have for a second time the saying about ears and hearing which Mark had earlier attached to the end of the parable, followed by the attachment formula, and two more sayings (vv. 24–25). These sayings are again reproduced by Matthew and Luke, but, as before, in different contexts. The two following parables are both introduced with a variation of the attachment formula (vv. 26, 30), and vv. 33–34 bring the whole session to a conclusion, repeating as a general rule (v. 34) something of which we saw one example (v. 10). The next story is also introduced with a variation of the attachment formula (v. 35) indicating that Mark is continuing to arrange the stories. Interestingly enough, from that point on, the stories are introduced without any form of the attachment formula. Apparently Mark found them already attached to each other. We will say more about that when we deal with the Markan miracle stories in the next chapter.

In summary, the teaching session contained in 4:1–34 is a parade example of the way Mark assembled independent traditions into a connected narrative. This is, as we saw, the longest teaching session Mark gives us. Surely we could expect its contents to provide us with further clues to the way Mark understood the teaching of Jesus.

All three of the parables, in one way or another, represent the contrast between beginnings and endings. The apparent failure of the sower who sees much of his seed ineffective is transformed into success by the incredible harvest. The tiny mustard seed provided, strangely enough, the largest shrub in the garden. The seed sowed and then ignored by the farmer, nevertheless, in unknown ways and by itself, produces the harvest he can then gather in. The four sayings in vv. 21–25 also, in different ways, contrast beginnings and endings. Lighting a lamp results in certain actions that are more appropriate than others; things that begin hidden end up manifest. The second pair of sayings tell about results determined by beginnings: the measure you give is the measure you get; those who start with much end with more, those with little end with less. There is much that could be said about the meaning of these sayings and parables in the pre-Markan tradition, and there are a number of studies that have undertaken that, but our major concern at this point is to get at Mark's understanding. How are these traditions related to one another in Mark's understanding of the career of Jesus?

One clue can be found in language so strange that both Matthew and Luke changed it, and English translations regularly do the same. V. 21 reads: "Surely a lamp does not come to be placed under basket or bed. Does it not rather come to be placed on a lampstand?" What kind of lamp is not brought, but "comes"? No lamp; clearly the language is figurative. But who comes as a lamp, though now it appears, contrary to one's normal expectation, that the light is hidden? Who has a beginning from which no one would suspect the final outcome? It is of course Jesus himself! The preceding two chapters in Mark are a story of Jesus being misunderstood by religious authorities (2:7, 16, 18, 24; 3:2, 6, 22) and even by his own family (3:21, 31). The significance of this Jesus, with whom God's kingdom dawns, nevertheless appears to be hidden. It is at this point not clear that his appearance is the dawning of God's glorious kingdom. Yet he cannot remain hidden; at the last, it will be apparent that the insignificance of his earthly ministry, rejected by authorities both during his life and at the end of it (e.g., 14:63–65), as well as by the crowds who in the end desert him (e.g., 15:12–14), will be vindicated by the glorious coming of the kingdom (e.g., 13:26; 14:62). What Jesus has begun will inevitably, by the power of God, result in the final harvest (e.g., 13:27). Thus parables and sayings alike point to one conclusion: insignificant though the earthly Jesus may appear, he is the beginning of God's final, glorious rule, and though his significance now appears to be hidden, it cannot remain that way. At the last he will be seen for what he truly is: the dawn of the rule of God.

If that is truly the case, however, then people ignore Jesus at their peril. For that reason they must listen carefully, lest they be confused by what Jesus says and lose what little religious understanding they have. Despite the fact that the beginning of God's rule in Jesus seems insignificant, great care must nevertheless be paid to him. One must listen to his every word, an activity that itself will reap great rewards in understanding. That of course is the point of the explanation of the parable (4:14–20). The entire force of that explanation is concentrated on the hearers. Not a word about who the sower is or what the seed is. With singleminded concentration the explanation centers on those who hear. Those who do not give complete attention will lose that word; those who hold fast to the end will be rewarded with their participation in the kingdom of God. It is not accidental that that very point is made in chap. 13, where Jesus speaks specifically about the final times (cf. 13:13b!). That is what this chapter of teaching is about: these seemingly ordinary times, which bring in their wake the extraordinary time of God's rule. Inexplicably, some refuse to see that fact. Inexplicably, while some accept, others reject Jesus and his words and deeds. Yet that is no different than it has always been: as with Jesus, so in earlier times people could look and just not see what was happening. They could hear and just not comprehend (cf. 4:12). For such people, Jesus' whole career was nothing but a parable dimly comprehended, and finally not at all. It is against such a fate that Mark has Jesus warn in this teaching session. Pay close attention to Jesus, Mark says, perhaps here echoing Jesus himself; what becomes of you in God's hands depends on how you react to this first light of his dawning kingdom.

Did Mark really intend such a unified interpretation of this collection of parables and sayings, or is this imposed upon him by the modern interpreter? Aside from the fact that such an interpretation explains why just this material would have been collected here, there is evidence in Mark's own language to lead to such a conclusion. It is clear from Mark's introduction to this chapter that he intends us to understand that we are getting a selection of examples from a much wider mass of material (cf. v. 2: "many parables"; "in the course of his teaching"). After the parable of the sower, Jesus' followers again ask "concerning the parables." Thus, Mark wants us to understand that the parable of the sower is exemplary of "the parables." That becomes explicit when this parable is identified as the key to all parables (v. 13). To understand this parable is thus to understand all parables, surely all of those included in the following verses. Yet just this parable and its two-fold explanation (vv. 11–12; 14–20) point clearly to the theme of the obscure, hidden beginning and the incredible, vindicating conclusions, and thus the need to pay careful, close attention. It is just this theme that finds amplification in the remaining material. Thus Mark himself seems to indicate the kind of unified interpretation we have found applicable to this whole "teaching session."

Furthermore, in 4:10–12, the disciples do not ask *why* Jesus speaks in parables; rather, they ask *concerning* them. The answer of Jesus in vv. 11 f. is then not an explanation of his teaching method, but of the content of the parable of the sower. The meaning of vv. 11 f. is the same as the second explanation (vv. 13–20), some understand, others do not, but here the content is cast in the form of the fulfillment of a prophetic oracle (Isa. 6:9–10). These verses do not give a psychological explanation of the rejection of Jesus; they simply demonstrate that the reaction to Jesus is typical of the reaction men characteristically give to the prophetic call to return to God: some respond, others reject.

The content of Jesus' teaching, therefore, is Jesus himself, just as the parable of the sower is the parable about parables, and the key to them all. The mystery of the kingdom given to Jesus' followers is also clearly Jesus himself. That Jesus and his fate are the content of Jesus' teaching is made explicit later in Mark's narrative, where Mark identifies as "teaching" the first two predictions by Jesus of his ultimate fate (8:31; 9:31). Even the identification of the puzzle about the relationship of Messiah to David as "teaching" (12:35) points in this direction, for Jesus, the Messiah, is precisely the one who raises the question about the Messiah. Even more, however, the total narrative in Mark confirms the point that these teachings in chap. 4 tell of Jesus himself. Time and again, those who hear Jesus are led to outright rejection of him and of what he says (e.g., 3:1–6, 22–30; cf. 4:15). Again and again, we hear the warning that some who follow Jesus will fall away when persecutions come (e.g., 13:12–13b; cf. 4:16–17). We hear Jesus' repeated warning that those who are preoccupied with riches are unable to take Jesus as seriously as he must be taken (e.g., 10:17–25; cf. 4:18–19). Finally, we hear again and again the promise that those who hold fast to Jesus and to his words will in the end find vindication (e.g., 10:29–30; 13:13b; cf. 4:20). The explanation of the parable of the sower is thus acted out in the career of Jesus; truly it is the key to all parables, because it is the key to the career of Jesus himself.

Above all, the disciples in Mark demonstrate the validity of the parable of the sower and of the teaching session as a whole. They themselves see the beginnings—and are confused. They themselves have the mystery of the kingdom, Jesus himself—and they waver. They themselves wonder at the hiddenness that will one day inevitably be clarified—and they fail. If they could see the glorious end that results from such beginnings, they would surely grasp the meaning of the whole career of Jesus, because, as the parables and sayings in chap. 4 make clear, it is only that glorious end that lets one see the beginning in its true and proper perspective. But is it ever possible to understand Jesus if all one sees is the beginning, or is that very impossibility precisely what the disciples in Mark demonstrate again and again? Is the end the only valid key to the beginning, without which one not only can, but must, *mis*understand Jesus? In that case, only the final events will make clear the meaning of Jesus. What those final events are, we will learn from Mark's narrative in due course. First we must consider some other elements that make up the career of Jesus.

CHAPTER EIGHT

*Power —
Kingdom
Peel*

JESUS AS MIRACLE WORKER

It is quite natural that the reader of Mark would gain the impression that among the important things Jesus did was the working of "miracles," or, as the Greek word for them would be better translated, "acts of power" (*dynameis*, the root of our word "dynamite"). More than any other of our four Gospels, Mark fills his narrative with stories of such acts by Jesus. In fact, the amount of space devoted to reports of miracles, in comparison to the length of the Gospels overall, declines as we move from Mark to Matthew and Luke, and then on to John. Mark thus devotes proportionately more space to the miracles of Jesus than any other document we have from the early Christian years. Some later "gospels" told many miracles of Jesus as a child, but stories of the wondrous deeds of the mature Jesus are pretty well exhausted in our canonical Gospels. Of those four, Mark devotes the most space to such accounts. Whatever else Mark may have thought about Jesus, he surely also understood him as one who performed acts of power.

It is also clear that Mark understood such acts of Jesus as a part of Jesus' combat against the forces of evil. This is apparent from the stories of exorcisms, where the possessing spirit is called a "demon," or is described as "unclean." The key to such an understanding is found at the end of a discussion Jesus had with some scribes about the kind of power he represented (3:22–27). In countering the charge that he was in league with Satan, and could thus dispel demons with Satan's permission, Jesus points out that if Satan permitted someone to destroy his own works, then his power would be coming to an end. Obviously, Jesus implies, Satan would not give power to one who would lessen Satan's power; if that were the case, Satan would be bent on self-destruction (vv. 24–26). Rather, Jesus says, he can cast out demons, not because he is a minion of Satan, but because he is stronger than Satan. Comparing his acts of power to plundering the realm of Satan's rule, Jesus says that could not happen unless the guardian of that realm were powerless to intervene. Such is in fact the case. The "strong man" has been rendered powerless, has been "bound," and so Jesus is free to plunder his realm (v. 27). Jesus' acts of power, particularly his exorcisms, thus demonstrate his mastery over Satan, and show to that extent at least that the power by which he acts is the power of God.

Yet the very fact that that kind of question could be raised by those who were witnesses to such acts points to the problem inherent in understanding the significance of those acts. A "miracle" in itself proves nothing at all about the one who performs it, least of all that that person is God's promised, anointed one who is the dawn of God's visible rule in the world. The Hellenistic world was full of wonder workers and magicians about whom marvelous tales were told. This was as true of the Jews as it was of the Greeks. A whole cluster of such stories are told of rabbis such as Hanina ben Dosa and Honi the Circle Maker: they healed the sick, overcame evil spirits, caused rain to start and stop, caused golden tables to materialize, and made ugly young ladies beautiful. Nor was the Greek world wanting in such stories. Stone tablets erected at the temple of the Greek god Asclepius at Epidauros contained story after story of the wondrous acts of that god: lame could walk, blind could see, the disfigured were healed, and chronic diseases were ameliorated or eliminated altogether. Even a pottery cup, accidentally broken by a slave, was miraculously restored after prayer to this Greek deity. That such stories were told about Jesus, therefore, did not set him apart from his age; they made him quite at home in it.

Even more, however, miracles are open to widely differing interpretations, ranging all the way from seeing in them evidence of God's power, to claiming they resulted from a magic trick. Miracles in themselves were ambiguous: to the faithful they were one more demonstration that confidence in Jesus as God's anointed is vindicated. To Jesus' opponents, such deeds simply furnish further proof that he must be done away with, because in him the forces of evil have found one more way to irrupt into God's creation. To the scribes from Jerusalem, they proved Jesus himself was demonic (3:22). To Jesus' friends and relatives, they proved Jesus was "beside himself," i.e., crazy (3:21). To the Pharisees, they were so inadequate that they had to be demonstrated in a form (probably with Jesus predicting the result, and then causing it to happen) that Jesus flatly refused (8:11–12). Even the disciples themselves, who had been participants in two of them (6:35–44; 8:1–9; although these are probably two parallel traditions Mark preserves them both), were unable to make any sense of them (8:17–18).

If, then, the primitive church were going to hand on the traditions about the mighty acts of Jesus, they ran the risk of telling accounts that at best were ambiguous, at worst capable of making Jesus appear to be just another of those wandering magicians so familiar to the Hellenistic world. Given those circumstances, the fact that such stories were preserved at all is perhaps the most persuasive evidence that Jesus did in fact do such things. The quickest solution to this problem would have been to concentrate on Jesus as teacher, and forget the specific accounts of his mighty deeds. In the later fathers that is just what happened.

Mark, however, did not ignore such stories. He used them, and in using them within his longer narrative he reinterpreted them, both by placing them at points in his narrative that gave them a different meaning than they apparently had had (e.g., 11:12–14, 20–21), and by providing them with an introduction, or a conclusion, or both, which pointed the story in a new direction (e.g., 1:21–27). Yet in doing that, Mark was simply continuing a process of interpreting these stories that had begun before him. We must examine that process of interpretation in more detail, if for no other reason than that it will frequently give the modern preacher a hint about how the Gospel authors understood those stories. They were as much a problem in the first century as they are in the twentieth, and any insight into those earlier solutions may help us in our solutions now.

Basically, the solution of the primitive church to the problem of the ambiguity inherent in any account of a mighty act was to build an interpretation into the structure of the miracle story itself. To understand how they did that, it is necessary to know something of the structure of a miracle story. Not surprisingly, the basic structure is one that is common to all stories of that kind: the *problem* is stated, the *solution* is given, and then some *proof* is cited that the solution in fact solved the problem. To the question how else one would tell such a story, the answer is simple: apparently no other way. Yet therein lies the point. Those are the elements which are necessary to tell the story; any further details, not necessary for such a story, must be accounted for in some other way than the desire simply to tell the story of a mighty act. It is important to remember here that none of the material in Mark is due to stenographic accounts by eyewitnesses. All material Mark had in his tradition had been passed on by word of mouth, and had to prove its usefulness in the primitive mission of the church, or it would not have been preserved. As miracle stories are told and retold, they just naturally assume the form we outlined above. Thus the structure of the stories of Jesus' mighty acts owe more to the way such a story must be told than to the way they actually happened.

That structure is elastic to the extent that each of the three elements may be expanded by details. Thus the *problem* may be stated at some length, with emphasis, for example, on how it has resisted solution up to now (e.g., 5:25–26). The *solution* may include a request for help, either by the sufferer (1:40) or by her friends or relatives (7:25–26), and may be recited in great detail (8:23–25a). The *proof* may include several indications that the problem has indeed been solved (5:42, 43b), and may also be expanded to include some reaction by the bystanders to show that they also recognized that the solution was genuine (7:37). Elastic though the structure may be, however, it is easy enough to tell whether or not individual details belong to the structure of the miracle story, or whether they constitute theologically interpretative additions to the story.

It is unclear whether such theologically interpretative details were ever included in the earliest form of the miracle stories of Jesus. It is possible that they may have been, but that seems less probable for two reasons. First, we have miracle stories included in Mark which have no such theological additions, indicating that stories could survive without them. In that case, they simply point to the power Jesus exercised in his earthly ministry. That in itself is, of course, a theological point, but as we saw, it is open to varying interpretations; that power could be from Satan as well as God. Secondly, as the tradition progresses the stories become more and more dominated by the theological interpretation. Thus, Luke and Matthew omit two of the three miracle stories Mark has that have no interpretative elements added to them, and Matthew consistently reshapes the stories to fit his own theological program. In John the interpretation tends to occupy far more space than the account of the miracle itself.

Thus, the likelihood is that most of the stories of Jesus' acts of power originated and were told without theological interpretation, perhaps among people who already shared the faith that the one who had done those things was their risen Lord. Later, to make them useful for purposes of teaching or preaching, theological interpretations had to be incorporated to make them less open to misunderstanding. In view of the way those stories were dealt with as they moved from the earlier to the later Gospels, such an explanation seems inherently more likely than that all began with such interpretations, which were later stripped off altogether, as would be the case with those three stories in Mark. It seems more probable that those three stories in Mark represent the final remnants of an original kind of story that increasingly underwent interpretation.

There were basically two ways to build in the theological interpretation. One was to add theological material to the story itself; the other was to give the story an interpretative framework. Some examples may help to demonstrate the points we are making.

The simplest, "pure" (i.e., uninterpreted) miracle story in Mark is the healing of Peter's mother-in-law (1:30–31). Perhaps because of its association with Simon Peter, this is the only uninterpreted miracle story Matthew and Luke take over from Mark. Two other unadorned miracle stories occur in Mark (8:22–26; 7:32–35, although this latter may have a rudimentary interpretation attached in vv. 36–37). Perhaps the clearest example of a theological insertion into a miracle story is found in 2:1–12. It is difficult to determine if Mark is responsible for this adaptation, or whether he found it in his tradition. Absence of clearly Markan constructions and vocabulary would lend weight to the supposition that the insertion occurred prior to the time Mark incorporated the story into his narrative. In this story, after Mark's sentence that makes it part of his ongoing narrative (v. 1), we have the *problem* (vv. 2–4a; the detail about the crowds compounds the problem of how the paralysed man will get to Jesus); the *solution* (vv. 4–5, 11; the repetition of the solution already indicates a later insertion into the story, as we shall see—digging through the roof is probably to be understood as an implied request for help); and the *proof* (v. 12; it includes a crowd reaction at the end to confirm that the healing in fact did take place, and in a wondrous way). In the middle of that story a dialogue occurs between Jesus and some scribes concerning whether or not Jesus has authority to forgive sins. Notice that the phrase "he said to the paralytic" is repeated verbatim in vv. 5 and 10, a clear sign that here the original story was interrupted. The first words of Jesus in v. 5b about forgiven sins belong to the interpretative insert to set the stage for the discussion; the words in v. 11 probably belong therefore to the original account of the healing. In that way, a story of a mighty act of Jesus has been turned into a discussion whose point is that the power that allows Jesus to heal also allows him to forgive sins, something important for Christians (like us!) who can no longer benefit directly from the physical presence of the healing Jesus, but who can still experience his power in the forgiveness of sin he offers. Other such theological insertions could be demonstrated, ranging from several verses (e.g., 3:1–5, where it includes vv. 2, 4–5a in a story of only five verses) to just a short phrase (e.g., 4:40, a question that turns a nature miracle into an implied story about the power of faith). A careful analysis of the miracle stories in Mark will enable one to isolate interpretative insertions in many other Markan miracle stories.

The second way, in addition to interpretative insertions, by means of which the tradition and Mark interpreted miracle stories was to put them within a framework which gives the story a theological point. We saw one example of this in the preceding chapter, when we considered the first miracle story in Mark (1:21–28). Here the framework interprets the miracle as an example of the power and authority Jesus also possessed when he taught. An analysis of vv. 23–27a will show that it is a regular miracle story, in this case an exorcism, in which the dialogue between the demoniac and Jesus constitutes part of the *problem*: by naming the exorcist, the demon normally acquired power over him. There are many other examples of miracle stories being interpreted by the framework into which they have been put, whether that framework surrounds the story, as in the case just discussed, or is restricted to an introduction (6:30–34) or a conclusion (6:52). Again, a careful analysis of the miracle stories in Mark will enable one to find the interpretative adaptation.

There is a third way, more difficult to analyse with any certainty and therefore more difficult to interpret, by means of which miracle stories were adapted, and that is by their combination. Mark 5:21–43 is an example of two miracle stories which have been combined in a very simple way. The story of the woman with the flow of blood (5:25–34) has simply been inserted into the story of the raising of Jairus' daughter (5:22–24a, 35–43), perhaps to let the statement about faith in the inner story interpret the meaning of the story into which it has been inserted. There is other evidence, however, largely the duplication of structural elements within a single miracle story, to indicate that at some pre-Markan stage in the tradition, two similar miracle stories could be combined into one. We know miracle stories could circulate as doublets, since Mark has preserved such a set of duplicate stories in 6:35–43 and 8:1–9. Perhaps other doublets were combined into one story at some point during their transmission. The stories that show such a duplication of structural elements are the story of the Gerasene demoniac (5:1–20); the story of Jesus walking on the sea (6:45–51, where one story seems to have been similar to the stilling of the storm found in 4:35–41, the other a story of Jesus walking on the sea); and the story of the healing of the possessed boy (9:14–27, where Mark has then added his own interpretative conclusion in vv. 28–29). Scholars have yet to solve the puzzle represented by such stories.

We have seen, then, how stories of the mighty acts of Jesus have been adapted in the course of their transmission, in order to indicate the direction in which their interpretation is to move. We have seen how Mark has continued that process of adaptation with individual stories. There is some indication of a further method by which miracle stories were adapted prior to Mark, and that was to put them into collections which could be used in some liturgical setting. There is evidence, literary and stylistic, that Mark found among his earlier traditions two collections of stories, each arranged according to a scheme that consisted of a miracle dealing with the sea, three healing miracles, and a wondrous feeding. Such an explanation seems the best way to explain the content and structure of Mark 4:35–8:26, with its recurrent patterns. If such collections existed, they probably represented the attempt by some primitive Christian community to give the miracles a eucharistic setting (the language of the feedings bears some similarity to the words of institution), thus providing them a larger interpretative setting. The point may have been that one had fellowship with Jesus the miracle worker when one shared in the eucharist, perhaps even to the point of taking some of his power into oneself. There is some evidence that that kind of interpretation of the eucharist did exist within the primitive church, and which, perhaps precisely because it downgraded the association of the eucharist with the suffering of Jesus on the cross, may have led to aberrations in eucharistic celebrations (cf. 1 Cor. 11:17–34, where Paul's corrective is a recitation of the institution of the eucharist in connection with Christ's death, not his wondrous power, v. 23b).

Whatever use may have been made earlier of these two collections of miracle stories, Mark incorporated them into his narrative, dissociated them from any eucharistic adaptation by working them into the Galilean portion of Jesus' ministry, and further reinterpreted them by inserting into each of them a large block of material which showed Jesus as one engaged in teaching and dispute. Into the first collection he inserted 6:1–33, which includes the implication, through the account of the death of John the Baptist, that Jesus would suffer a similar fate. Into the second collection Mark inserted 7:1–23, showing Jesus as teacher in dispute with Jewish religious leaders (the two insertions show repeated Markan constructions and vocabulary; the surrounding miracle stories do not). Mark has also adapted the stories in the collections by giving some of them, at least, a different geographic distribution (e.g., 7:24, 31), thus using the stories for different purposes than they apparently served in the earlier collections.

In such ways, therefore, Mark continued the process of adapting and interpreting the miracle stories, a process which had been part of the traditioning of this material for some time before Mark began his writing, and which continued when his material was incorporated into Matthew and Luke. Thus the wonder working Jesus was incorporated into a faith that experienced his continued presence with his followers after the resurrection, and the stories of his mighty acts were interpreted to bring that faith to expression. The stories were shaped, therefore, to show that the power which could perform such wonders during Jesus' earthly career was still present for those who, through their faith in him, incorporated themselves into a fellowship whose Lord he continued to be.

There is a further concept which has often been associated with Mark's reinterpretation of the miracle traditions he found in the materials available to him, a concept which is popularly described with the term "messianic secret." This term appeared first in the book by William Wrede (*The Messianic Secret*, 1901), who observed that Jesus repeatedly commands people not to tell what he had done (5:43; 7:36; 1:44) or who he was (1:34; 3:11–12; 8:30; 9:9). Furthermore, the disciples, who heard and saw what Jesus said and did, failed to understand either what he said or who he was, despite repeated private instruction. Yet if Jesus really had wanted to remain unknown, what better way than to do or say nothing? Wrede asked: what is the meaning of this kind of evidence? Taking his cue from the emphasis on the importance of Jesus' resurrection and the clear implication that only then did people understand who and what Jesus was, Wrede argued that all references to Jesus as Messiah came from the post-Easter period of the church. Further, Wrede argued, the reason the church only then realized who Jesus was was due to the fact that up to that point there was no hint that he was Messiah. Jesus, said Wrede, never thought of himself as Messiah; only after Easter did that idea arise. Yet when Christians tried to come to terms with their recollections of Jesus' non-messianic career in light of the post-Easter messianic faith, they faced the problem of accounting for Jesus' life in light of their faith. If he were Messiah, would he not have known it, and would it not have become evident? To answer "yes," Wrede said, the idea was developed that Jesus was Messiah, but wanted that to be kept secret. Such an idea would explain why more people did not recognize he was Messiah, despite his miracles, and would also explain why in Mark's narrative Jesus did not openly proclaim his status, and tried to keep others from telling it. That is also why, according to Wrede, the disciples are portrayed as never having fully understood Jesus: in his desire to keep himself and his status secret, he kept the disciples from full understanding. Wrede sought to buttress his arguments by pointing to the fact that injunctions to secrecy accompany miracles (including the transfiguration) which, in his view, cannot have been historical events, and thus the nonhistorical origin of the messianic secret was supported.

Wrede's thesis has loosed a continuing debate which has failed to result in any unanimity among scholars up to the present. It is clear that Mark's problem was not to impose a messianic view of Jesus on a non-messianic tradition. His tradition held Jesus to be Messiah from as far back as we can trace it. Nor are Wrede's observations about injunctions to silence accurate. As often as Jesus specifically commands silence about a miracle (5:43; 7:36), he commands or allows the miracle to be told abroad (5:19–20; 10:52). By far the largest majority of miracle stories have no word about secrecy one way or the other (e.g., 2:12; 3:5; 4:41; 5:34; 6:44, 51; 8:10; 9:27) and Jesus' command to secrecy could be deliberately violated (7:36). Obviously, such evidence could hardly account for a Jesus who wanted to remain hidden. Some evidence Wrede took to refer to secrecy we now know is not intended that way; for example, the command to the demon to be silent (1:25) is part of the defensive language an exorcist used to protect himself against a counterspell by the demon. Its use in 4:39 (the same Greek words) where there is no question of secrecy also confirms this. Again, while Mark does interpret Jesus' command to silence to the demons as Jesus' effort to avoid their confession of him as "Son of God" (3:11–12; cf. also 1:34, where 1:25 is interpreted as command to secrecy), he is not at all consistent in doing so. Time and again, there are references to demonic expulsions where there is no mention of secrecy, whether in miracle stories (7:30; 9:27) or in summaries (1:39; 6:30).

Furthermore, remarks about secrecy disobeyed (e.g., 1:45; 7:36), together with such verses as 7:24 and 9:30, where Jesus' desired secrecy cannot be obtained, belong to the motif of the enormous popularity awakened by Jesus, and the great popular acceptance he enjoyed in Galilee (e.g., 1:28, 37; 2:13; 3:7–9; 4:1; 5:21). They have nothing to do with any secrecy motif in the sense Wrede spoke of it; they have to do rather with Jesus' popularity. Perhaps Mark wants to contrast the crowds in Galilee that accepted Jesus with those in Jerusalem who rejected him (15:11, 13–15, 29).

Finally, the command to the disciples not to tell anyone that he was the Christ (8:30), like the command to Peter, James, and John not to divulge the transfiguration, owe more to Mark's theological understanding of the climax and key to Jesus' career than they do to any historical reminiscence, or to any attempt to account for absence of knowledge of the earthly Jesus as Messiah. The key to those passages is surely the temporal condition affixed to the prohibition in

9:9; only after the resurrection can such events be narrated or such confessions be made with any possibility of their being correctly meant by those who spoke them or understood by those who heard them.

Any attempt to deal with the "messianic secret" in Mark, therefore, is first obliged to differentiate between the kinds of secrecy materials Mark provides, and the varying theological and narrative motifs they represent. Only in that way can Mark's intention be elicited. Wrede's basic error lay in trying to reduce all such phenomena in Mark to a single common denominator.

One final point: it is not accidental, surely, that of all the miracle stories available to him, Mark chose to place first of all the miracle which interpreted Jesus' teaching as sharing the power of his mighty acts (1:21–28). In that way, Mark has provided us the key to his reinterpretation of the miracles of Jesus: the power at work in Jesus in those mighty acts was—and is—at work in his words. Perhaps that is in the end what led Mark to decide to write an account of those words and those deeds: in them the power of Jesus is still available. In that fact surely there would be justification for Mark to undertake the new literary venture upon which he embarked.

CHAPTER NINE

THE PASSION OF JESUS

It is evident that the final few days of Jesus' life occupy an inordinate amount of space in Mark's narrative compared to the space devoted to the remainder of his public career. Even if the events of Jesus' career, as they are narrated in Mark, need only have filled the space of a few months (the idea of a three-year public career for Jesus is drawn from the Gospel of John, and is quite foreign to Mark and the other two synoptic Gospels), the amount of space Mark devotes to the final week would still be disproportionately large. That fact alone would be enough to give us some indication of the importance Mark attached to these events. For that reason, it has become common, since the phrase was coined around the beginning of this century by Martin Kaehler, to refer to the Gospel of Mark as a passion narrative with an extended introduction.

More has come to be implied in that statement, however, than merely a reference to the disproportionate amount of narrative space Mark gives to those events, or even to the fact that this represents the climax of his Gospel. There is a widespread view that while Mark found the pre-passion traditions in isolated form, or at most in small collections, he found the passion story essentially complete and in its present sequence. Thus, it is concluded, while Mark has been free to shape the material in the first ten, or even the first thirteen chapters, he is bound to the tradition in chapters fourteen and fifteen, and has not shaped them so freely as he did the preceding material in accord with his own theological understanding. Further, all four Gospels agree in general regarding the events surrounding Jesus' crucifixion, pointing to a common pre-Markan narrative. Finally, since in Mark the material, contrary to his normal practice, is given in a sequential account covering seven days, the general conclusion has been drawn that the account of Jesus' passion is the oldest continuous narrative in the gospel traditions. Mark, therefore, so it is believed, took individual stories, and perhaps some small collections of stories, and fashioned them into an introduction to the already formulated passion story that was circulating within the primitive church. The conclusion was further drawn, on occasion, that if that were the case, then these narratives also had strongest claim to historical validity.

Some scholars are now beginning to insist, however, that that consensus must be carefully re-examined, and the re-examinations undertaken to date have done little to confirm such a view of the Markan passion story. In fact, the results have all pointed in the opposite direction. Analysis of the Markan narrative, and of the passion narratives in the other Gospels, leads to the same kind of conclusions that earlier analysis of the preceding narrative in Mark had led, namely, Markan editorial work is as surely evident in this part of his Gospel as in earlier parts.

Further study of the passion narrative in Matthew and Luke has also shown that each of them recasts the passion story in conformity with his own theological conceptions. That simply means that the unity between their accounts and that of Mark is no greater and no less than their agreement in any other place where Luke and Matthew follow Mark. They follow Mark's order, but add other material and recast the Markan narrative to give it the point they feel appropriate. There is no indication, therefore, from the way in which Matthew and Luke make use of the Markan passion narrative that they were aware of a generally accepted, pre-Markan formulation of those events. A consideration of the passion story in John reveals major differences. John has the temple cleansing at the very outset of Jesus' ministry instead of during the last week. In its place John put the story of the raising of Lazarus and makes it a major motivation for the death of Jesus. John has no eucharistic institution, no prayer in Gethsemane, and, like the other Gospels, differing last words of Jesus on the cross. The agreement between John and the synoptics consists largely in the fact that they contain stories about the trial, Peter's denial, condemnation by Pilate, crucifixion between two thieves, and burial by Joseph of Arimethea. These few similar stories are presented in John in language different from that used in the synoptic accounts, however, thus pointing to their existence in a common fund of early tradition, rather than in the form of a coherent narrative. They may have appeared in the tradition in barest outline form, perhaps in not much more detail than that just used to outline them.

Up to now, the arguments advanced for the position that Mark exercised as much compositional freedom on individual traditions in his account of the last days of Jesus' career as he did in his earlier account, have appeared almost exclusively in doctoral dissertations or post-doctoral studies subsequently published in English and in German. They are of a highly technical nature, and are written for fellow scholars. It may therefore be helpful, since these arguments are not readily available, to summarize some of the evidence they rely upon, in order to pose the problem. It promises to be a problem that will continue to be discussed, and which has profound theological implications for our understanding of areas ranging from the possibility of recovering the historical Jesus to assessing Mark's place as a creative influence on the shape of our faith. It is therefore a problem worth pursuing.

A careful examination of the structure of Mark 11–16 reveals the seven day format within which Mark casts his material, but it also reveals enough uncertainties to lead the reader to wonder if this was a normative structure Mark inherited, which exercised a limiting and binding influence on his narrative; or a scheme Mark wanted to impose on his material to give it some kind of organization; or merely a convenient way to connect some very diverse material, as he had done earlier in his narrative with certain indications of the passage of days (e.g., 1:32, 35; 4:35; 6:2, 47).

Jesus' week in Jerusalem would have to begin with his approach to the city in 11:1, a day which is regarded as having ended after 11:11 (1st day). The second day begins explicitly with 11:12, and ends explicitly at 11:19 (2nd day). The third day begins, rather clearly, with 11:20, but there is no mention of its end. If we assume that the next mention of time in 14:1 signals the beginning of a new day, we end up with eight rather than seven days between triumphal entry and empty tomb on Easter morning. If, in order to arrive at a seven day scheme, we end the third day and begin the fourth with 14:12, we must simply ignore 14:1. There is a further difficulty here. 14:12 identifies the "first day of Unleavened Bread" with the day "they sacrificed the passover lamb," yet the former is the 15th Nisan, the latter the 14th Nisan (the Jewish month during which Passover was celebrated). Perhaps, as some evidence indicates, the day the lamb was slain was popularly known as the first day of Unleavened Bread, i.e., the first day of Passover, but if that is the case, then the chronology is completely confused by the reference in 14:1 to it being *two* days before "the Passover and the feast of the Unleavened Bread." Such a mistake in chronology would be easiest to explain if Mark were trying to fit independent traditions together each of which had some specific designation of time (as did the story of the transfiguration, 9:2). It is difficult to explain if Mark sees a seven day period as important, and almost impossible to explain if one assumes an earlier pre-Markan narrative which reflected actual historical events.

If, for the sake of the seven day scheme, we assume the end of the third day and the beginning of the fourth with 14:12, that day would end at 14:72, since with 15:1 the fifth day begins. That day ends with the account of the burial of Jesus, identified in 15:42 as the day before the sabbath. Again there is a problem if we assume the Jewish method of reckoning the day from sunset to sunset, since the language with which 15:42 begins seems to designate the end of one day and the beginning of the next. If the day before the sabbath did not begin until that evening, we have nine days altogether, with two of them passed over in silence (the day before the sabbath and the sabbath). If Mark does not intend us to understand days as reckoned from sunset to sunset (Jewish mode) but from midnight to midnight (Roman mode), which would allow 15:42 to fit the seven day scheme, it means that this tradition at least was shaped after the time that the traditions passed into gentile, Greek-speaking areas. The third possibility would be simply that Mark was not intent on any time scheme, and thus could permit himself a general time designation ("when evening had come," as in 1:32, a Markan summary composition; also 4:35) to introduce an independent tradition that carried with it its own time designation. The sixth day is passed over in silence, on any reckoning, between 15:47 and 16:1, where it then becomes the day after the sabbath, thus the seventh day.

If to such a quick survey of evidence one adds the fact that neither Matthew nor Luke felt bound to the temporal format within which Mark presented his material—they try, without conspicuous success, to clarify some of the more difficult passages—it becomes clear that they felt free to ignore it, as they ignored Mark's other temporal sequences in the preceding narrative. Either that or they simply could not recognize the seven day scheme, in which case its existence may be clearer in the minds of some interpreters of Mark than it is in Mark's own narrative. In any case, the "last week" of Jesus in Jerusalem must remain a general designation (7 days? 8? even 9?), not an exact chronological definition.

Aside from such considerations, which have long posed problems for scholars who seek to understand Mark, there is increasing evidence emerging from close scrutiny of these chapters that much of this material existed independently, and has for the first time been combined by Mark.

It has long been recognized that a good deal of this material shows the same indications of independent circulation as does the earlier material. Such stories as Jesus' conflicts with various religious authorities in the temple (11:27–33; 12:13–34) seem to be as "rounded off" as the similar stories in 2:1–3:6, and thus could have circulated independently of any context. A similar judgment is possible about other episodes such as 12:35–37 and 41–44. Similarly, the story of the anointing of Jesus in Bethany (14:3–9), the parable of the wicked tenants (12:1–11), and perhaps the account of the preparations for the last supper (14:12–16), as well as the words of institution themselves (14:22–25) could, in their present form, have circulated independently of their present context in Mark. We know from 1 Cor. 11:23–25, for example, that an account of the words of institution did circulate that way.

Furthermore, a careful study of the narrative of the events of Jesus' final days recorded in Mark 14–15 reveals enough indications of the kind of editorial work also found in the material contained in the first ten chapters to lead one to conclude that both sections were shaped in the same way. Whatever judgments one makes about the first ten chapters ought also to be made about these last chapters. For example, the story of Jesus' anointing in Bethany (14:3–9) is rounded off, and shows the marks of an "anecdote." Even with the conclusion in v. 9 which points to Jesus' death, it need not have circulated in the context of Jesus' last days; references to Jesus' impending death have been strewn through Mark's narrative since 3:6. In fact, Mark introduced the story with just such a general statement about the desire of the religious authorities to do away with Jesus (cf.

3:6; 11:18; 12:12), and concluded it with the general information that the betrayer was now seeking his opportunity.

In a similar way, 14:12 and 17 seem to be the kind of editorial framing Mark has been employing from the beginning of his narrative, in order to give coherence to independent traditions. Again, the unnecessary second reference to the meal in 14:22 (we know that already from 14:18) indicates v. 22 began an independent tradition, which carried in itself enough indication of circumstance to make it understandable. Some scholars have suggested that Mark composed Mark 14:17–20, repeating the theme of the betrayer begun in vv. 10–11, to introduce the previously independent saying about the Son of man in v. 21.

The words of institution also present a problem, since 14:25 seems unconnected to vv. 22–24. V. 25 speaks only of the cup, ignoring the bread, and it implies that Jesus shared at least in the cup, something quite foreign to vv. 22–24. Further, the implication of vv. 22–24 seems to be that the disciples already share in the eschatological fulfillment of the covenant, while v. 25 may intend to say that the real fulfillment lies in the future, when Jesus returns and the kingdom of God is a reality in the world. If such an eschatological "reservation" is intended, Mark may have wanted to tone down an overly enthusiastic celebration of the eucharist both by linking it to Jesus' death (by putting it in this context), and by deemphasizing any present sharing in Jesus' power by substituting a future anticipation of Christ's return in God's kingdom. That is just what Paul did in 1 Cor. 11 when he added the reference to the time (v. 23) and to Jesus' eventual return (v. 26). Perhaps Paul and Mark, independently of one another, are combatting a widespread abuse of the Lord's supper.

The next passage, with the Markan attachment formula (14:27), and the continuation of the Markan theme of the failure of the disciples, is due to Mark's compositional activity. 14:30 is directly tied to the Markan formulation of Peter's denial; both Matthew and Luke omit the awkward reference to the cock crowing twice. That this is a literary formulation is hardly to be doubted; it is difficult to believe Peter would not remember this prophecy until the cock had crowed a *second* time. Surely the first sound of the cock, in the midst of such denials, would have been sufficient, as Matthew and Luke both assumed.

Prayer

The account of the prayer in Gethsemane is replete with Markan constructions and attachment formulae, so that there can be little question that this passage in its present form owes a great deal to Markan literary activity. The traditions themselves may have been associated with Jesus' arrest, and thus with his passion (esp. vv. 35–40), but Mark has assembled the material, and has introduced it with v. 32, so that the announced goal of v. 26 (the Mount of Olives) is reached. These verses are the final preparation of Jesus' passion before it begins. They also continue the regular and repeated Markan theme of the failure of the disciples, and show them incapable of emulating Jesus' acceptance of his God-willed suffering.

With 14:32, Mark begins his narrative of the events of Jesus' passion. All elements that had been predicted through the course of the narrative up to this point are fulfilled, and there can be little question, on that basis alone, that Mark sees these events as the climax of Jesus' career. Aside from v. 50, which is the final act of failure on the part of the disciples, to which Mark has pointed from the outset of his story, the material in 14:43–52 appears traditional. It contains information unnecessary for the reader of this context (e.g., Judas was one of the 12, v. 43; cf. 14:10, 17–18), but necessary in an independent tradition, and the resistance of Jesus' followers (v. 47) contrasts sharply with the Markan notation about their behavior.

Trial

The trial scene, contained in 14:53–72, also shows clear indications that it has been assembled by Mark. In a detailed study devoted to these verses, Prof. J. R. Donahue (*Are You the Christ?*) has made a strong case for the view that this segment of Mark, as all the material preceding it, has been constructed by Mark from independent traditions, which he has assembled, using familiar linguistic constructions and compositional techniques. For example, the trial of Jesus (vv. 55–65) has been inserted into the account of Peter's denial, a way of using traditions quite typical of Mark. Again, the trial scene has two motifs: witnesses who disagree in their statements that Jesus said he would destroy the temple (vv. 56–59) and Jesus' christological confession (v. 62) which the high priest says is blasphemous and which precipitates Jesus' final fate (vv. 63–65). These motifs are unrelated, and although a further reference to Jesus' statement about the destruction of the temple is found in 15:29, it plays no further part in the condemnatory proceedings against Jesus (for Mark's version of what Jesus actually said, cf. 13:2, both Mark 14:57–58 and 15:29 are closer to the tradition in John 2:19, reflected in Acts 6:14, than to anything in the Markan narrative). Donahue suggests that vv. 56–59 may be the result of a Christian meditation (a "pesher") on the fate of Jesus as reflected in Pss. 27:12 or 35:11, where, as in Isaiah 53, the motif of accusation by unjust witnesses is found, a meditation which Mark here incorporated into the actual trial scene. Be that as it may, the framework of the trial scene (vv. 53b, 55, 65) shows traits of Markan composition, indicating that this episode may also be due, in its present shape, to Mark. Thus, it appears that Mark took individual traditions dealing with witnesses unjustly accusing the innocent Jesus, a christological confession by Jesus, the denial of Peter, and some other traditions about Jesus' fate at the hands of Jewish officials, and combined them into a coherent narrative. Whether or not, therefore, there was a previous tradition about the trial of Jesus, the story as it now stands in Mark shows every indication of being due to his own editorial framing. If he did not create it, he surely gave it its present shape and thrust by the way he combined and connected the traditions.

It is for that reason, of course, that the "trial" is so difficult to justify in terms of Jewish law and customs, and why scholars have been unable to agree on whether it followed valid Jewish legal precedent or not. The reason is simply that in its present form, the story is not a court stenographer's report, but a theological witness to the suffering Christ, who will come again in glory, who was rejected and abused by those who ought to have welcomed him as the anointed one they so fervently yearned to see. It is therefore idle to argue about "legality" when the traditions have been shaped by an author whose purpose simply did not include such consideration.

The fifteenth chapter, with its accounts of the further fate of Jesus, yields the same results to literary and form critical analysis as did chapter fourteen. Markan constructions occur within the narrative material (e.g., vv. 1, 8, 18, 22), and the typically Markan stylistic form of the so-called "kai-parataxis" (using the conjunction "and"—kai—to introduce a sentence) occurs at least twenty-five times. It would seem that the conclusion to which we came about chapter fourteen will also have to be reached about chapter fifteen: it owes its present form to the redactional activity of Mark. Finally, scholars have long been persuaded that chapter sixteen, although not composed by Mark, was adapted by him for his narrative, and attached to the end of the account of Jesus' death.

There is good evidence, therefore, to assume that Mark, rather than providing an extended introduction to an already formulated account of Jesus' suffering and death, composed and arranged his entire narrative from independent traditions, which he skillfully connected by appropriate if minimal literary activity. That conclusion of course does nothing to weaken the impression that Jesus' death was for Mark the climax of Jesus' career. On the contrary, it strengthens it. It means that Mark wrote his Gospel in such a way that the historical climax of Jesus' career now became its theological climax as well. Theme after theme which occurred throughout the Gospel— Jesus' conflict with religious authorities, the lack of understanding displayed by his disciples, the suffering and death he himself repeatedly predicted—here reached their fulfillment. The cross therefore not only *ends* the career of Jesus, it also represents its *culmination*, and the key to its meaning. If Mark is in fact responsible for the formulation of the scenes about Jesus' last days in Jerusalem, as well as the preceding times in Galilee, then the meaning of Jesus, which is ultimately found in his passion and for which Paul had earlier struggled, has now achieved narrative clarification and legitimation. Now, for the first time, the individual traditions about Jesus were given a coherence whose climax and fulfillment were Jesus' passion and death. Here is the key to the Markan reinterpretation of the Jesus tradition. Now all of the disparate individual stories and sayings which circulated about Jesus found an interpretative framework within which they could be understood. The success of Mark's attempt at reinterpretation can be measured by the ease with which both Matthew and Luke were able to integrate into that framework additional material about which Mark either was ignorant, or which he chose not to include. But from the time of Mark forward, the story of Jesus—indeed, *any* story about Jesus—could not be told except within the interpretative framework that saw in his death the climax of his theological significance as well as of his earthly career.

But what of the resurrection? The Gospel ends with an empty tomb and some fearful women. There has been a good deal of speculation on the possibility that Mark did not end in the form we now have it, with 16:8, but went on to include accounts of the appearances of the risen Jesus. Some have suggested parts of John 21, which was apparently added after the first twenty chapters of that Gospel were completed, may be the "lost ending" which a later editor then attached to John rather than Mark. Yet the earliest manuscripts we have of Mark end with 16:8, and if Mark included no accounts of the risen Jesus, neither did he mention his pre-existence or his birth. The further fact that Matthew and Luke, who follow Mark rather closely in their accounts of Jesus' suffering and death, diverge so widely from one another in their accounts of Jesus' appearance on Easter, make it apparent that their copy of Mark omitted such accounts as well. It would thus seem more appropriate to attempt to understand Mark's Gospel in the earliest form we know it, rather than to try speculatively to "complete" his story for him.

However that question be resolved, there can be no question that Mark knew Jesus rose from the dead. Not only are there repeated references to that event in the course of his narrative, but there is also the announcement in 16:6–7 that Jesus has in fact risen. Why then does Mark not include stories of Jesus' appearances? Did he not know of them? Yet two or three decades earlier, Paul knew of a tradition about such appearances (1 Cor. 15:3–7), so they were already by that time widespread. What was it that made such overwhelming emphasis on the suffering Jesus important enough to cause Mark to omit accounts of the resurrection which he obviously knew had happened? We can, of course, only guess at the answers to such questions, but perhaps closer consideration of the way Mark portrayed Jesus' followers, particularly his closest disciples, will give us some clues to an answer.

why did Mark know ___ of Resurrect (1Cor 15)
yet chose to forgo relating?

CHAPTER TEN

THE DISCIPLES IN MARK

If there is any progression in the picture Mark paints of the disciples, it appears to be from bad to worse. Their lack of understanding (beginning with chap. 4 and extending through 8:26) becomes their misunderstanding (8:27–10:45), by virtue of which they consistently fail to see what Jesus is trying to tell them about his own fate. That has as its consequence their utter failure in following him as that fate overtakes him (11:1–14:72). Can that be an accurate historical picture of the behavior of the twelve? If it is, one wonders how the Jesus traditions ever began. After all, it is precisely those traditions which show the disciples' *lack* of understanding; surely that presumes understanding at some point, in the light of which the former attitude was recognized as one of failure to understand. Later tendencies to glorify the disciples (even in Matthew and Luke they fare better, on the whole, than they do in Mark) make it unlikely that such traditions were purely the invention of the primitive church. The memory of utter failure on the part of those close followers of Jesus has the ring of painful truth about it. Yet, as we shall see, that failure becomes so important in Mark's Gospel that it clearly reflects part of the interpretative design into which he fit those earlier independent traditions about Jesus.

Could it be that in fact this treatment of the disciples provides us the key to an understanding of the purpose and point of this Gospel? Some scholars have come to that conclusion. In this understanding of Mark, the disciples become the spokesmen for a view of Jesus that Mark finds unacceptable (a view of Jesus as a Hellenistic "divine man," a wonder worker) and so he writes his Gospel to show that Jesus himself rejected such an interpretation by rejecting the disciples who are made to reflect such a Christology (T. J. Weeden, *Mark— Traditions in Conflict*). Thus, again and again, the disciples show

how such an understanding of Jesus was rejected by Jesus himself and led to failure on their part really to comprehend what Jesus was about. The disciples are thus pictured in Mark as representatives of the "heresy" that made Mark's Gospel necessary. Such a view probably goes too far in making the closest followers of Jesus the representatives of such a heresy, in view of the dependence of the later church on those very disciples for the traditions about Jesus. Unless some, or all, of the twelve stood behind the position Mark supposedly found so reprehensible in the community for which he wrote his Gospel, it is difficult to see why Mark would single them out as representatives of that pernicious view. In light of a lack of evidence for that point, Weeden's thesis as a whole is difficult to credit. We know there were disputes among the twelve, and among other close followers of Jesus (Acts 10–15 and Galatians 2 make that clear enough), but there is no indication that all the twelve were regarded as totally erroneous.

If such an interpretation of the role of the disciples in Mark's Gospel seems to carry evidence too far, one nevertheless cannot deny that the picture Mark paints of the disciples is not a flattering one. Time and again, despite private explanations (4:10, 34; 7:17; 9:28; 10:10), they betray their inability to grasp what is going on about them (e.g., 4:13; 6:52; 7:18; 8:17; 9:32). They say things that show their total lack of comprehension of what Jesus tried to tell them (e.g., 8:32; 10:38), and they confirm their failure when in the critical moment they all desert him. They have thus not only misunderstood, they have rejected what they have seen.

To be sure, the disciples are not the only ones who are pictured as failing to comprehend what was happening in Jesus of Nazareth. From beginning to end, Jesus is opposed in Mark's Gospel, and his teachings rejected by the Jewish religious authorities. Throughout the whole narrative, Pharisees oppose and plot against him, an activity shared by scribes and priests (e.g., 2:7; 3:6; 8:11; 10:2; 11:18; 12:12; 14:1; 15:31). They oppose what he does and what he says, and plot to kill him after their first encounter with him (3:6). Their opposition is understandable. Jesus represents a threat to all they hold to be true: the law as they understand it (e.g., 7:1–13). More than that, Jesus responds to their rejection of him with harsh language (7:6, 9; 12:9, 38), and is uncompromising in his opposition to the position they represent. He allows no room for possible error in his own position, and by implication little if any room for truth in theirs. It is with such people that Mark associates the disciples when he portrays their characteristic inability to understand Jesus, who he is, and what he teaches.

There are of course times when they are shown in a more positive light. The account of the calling of the disciples (1:16–20), placed as it is in Mark before any of the mighty acts of Jesus that might have given them stronger motivation to follow him (contrast Luke 4:31–5:11), put them in a positive light. They did in fact abandon all things to follow Jesus. When they reminded him of that fact (10:28), Jesus in no way denied it, but assured them they would have their reward. Perhaps the fact that they followed him as long as they did puts them in something of a positive light: despite their inability to understand everything Jesus said and did, they did stay with him. The ambiguity of their position is demonstrated, however, by the positive way in which Mark pictures other groups responding to Jesus. Two may be singled out. First, the crowds that surrounded him are regularly portrayed in Mark as responding in an enthusiastically positive way. Not only is this the case with the crowds in Galilee (e.g., 1:27–28; 2:2; 3:7; 4:1; 5:21; 6:34; 7:37; 8:1; 10:1) but also in Jerusalem (e.g., 11:9; 12:37). Second, Mark seems to go out of his way to portray some women as responding positively to Jesus (e.g., 5:28; 7:25; 14:3). In marked contrast to the twelve, the women who followed Jesus from Galilee to Jerusalem remained faithful to the end (contrast 15:40–47 with 14:50). It is they who alone are left to tend the buried corpse of Jesus (16:1), and they who are the first to learn of the empty tomb. In light of their faithfulness around the cross, it is highly unlikely that Mark intended the reader to think that as a result of their fearful reaction to such news (16:8) they disobeyed the angelic message to inform the disciples. There may be an intended note of irony here: the women must proclaim the good news of Jesus' resurrection to the disciples before the latter can embark on their own task of proclamation.

However we may want to judge that, it is clear that Mark did not understand the ministry of Jesus in such a way that it was totally open to rejection and misunderstanding. There is a further point to be made, however. It is clear from the way Mark has constructed his narrative that not only did the disciples fail to understand, but in one instance, at least, they had no possibility of understanding. Their hearts were hardened (6:52; cf. 8:17). What could Mark have meant with such a remark? We have already seen, in our discussion of 11:11–25, that the remark about the time for figs (11:13) is best explained as a reference to God's plan which works itself out in Jesus, and through the church which grows out of Jesus' career. Mark has other instances of such a divine plan. Scholars have long recognized the "divine necessity" contained in the "must" (e.g., "the Son of man *must* suffer many things," 8:31; see also 9:11), which Mark has put into his report of certain events. That same kind of divine necessity is reflected in passages that speak of the necessity of the fulfillment of "what is written" (e.g., 9:12; 14:21). Is this the kind of thinking that informs the remark about the hardening of the disciples' hearts? We may be in a position to answer that question a little further on.

For the moment, however, it has become clear that the picture Mark paints of the disciples is a complex one. Any solution that wants to do justice to Mark's understanding of and purpose for his narratives concerning them will have to take this complexity into account. There is one figure among the disciples who stands out from the rest, and in whom that complexity comes clearly to the fore. That figure is Simon Peter, and an examination of his role in Mark's narrative may help throw further light on the way Mark wants us to understand the role of the disciples.

There can be no question that Mark assigns to Peter a leading role among the disciples. He is the first one to be called (1:16), his is the first name on the list of the twelve, and he is the first one who is renamed by Jesus (3:16; prior to this point, he is always referred to as "Simon"; after this point, he is called "Peter" with the minor exception of 14:37). He is always the first one named of an inner circle of disciples (5:37; 9:2; 13:3; 14:33) and he frequently functions as spokesman for the group in both positive and negative ways (1:36; 8:29; 9:5–6; 10:28; 11:21). Peter's is the only denial that Jesus foretells explicitly (14:29–31), his is the only one narrated in detail (14:66–72), and he is the only disciple who is named when the women are instructed to tell the disciples that Jesus has risen and has gone before them to Galilee (16:7). In addition, Peter is the only one of the twelve to have had a member of his family healed (1:29–31); he stayed with Jesus longer during his trial than any other disciple Mark tells us about; and he is the only one whose repentance at his desertion of Jesus is reported (14:72). Clearly, Peter plays a key role among the disciples in Mark.

In light of that fact, it is instructive to note that his role is by no means limited to positive words and acts. If he is the spokesman for the group, he expresses the worst as well as the best (e.g., 8:29; 9:5–6). If he is the first to be called, his rejection of Jesus is heightened by his repeated denials that he would ever desert him in a time of trial. But if he is the one who bears the brunt of Jesus' wrath (8:33; Peter alone among the twelve is thus associated with satanic opposition to Jesus), he is also the one whom the angel singles out by name to be informed that Jesus is risen from the dead. If he is the only one singled out by name for rebuke of the three who slept while Jesus prayed (14:37), he is also the one the church remembered as first to be named when the twelve were tolled (3:16). Thus Peter stands out as the one who seems to represent the twelve, both in their faithfulness and perceptiveness, as well as in their faithlessness and lack of understanding. There is no indication that he was better or worse than any other member of the group that associated with Jesus, but clearly the disciples seem to find their representative figure in him.

It would appear to be wrong, therefore, to see in Mark an attempt to denigrate Peter. His failings are the failings of the group; it is just that Peter is painted with bolder strokes and with more vivid color. It would appear to be equally wrong to see in Mark exclusively an attempt to rehabilitate a Peter whose reputation in some circles was in doubt. If Peter emerges in the end with at least the potentiality of becoming a "hero of the faith," so do the remaining disciples, with the conspicuous exception of Judas, the betrayer. Whatever Mark wanted to say about Peter, he clearly wanted to say about the disciples as a group, both as the twelve, and as a smaller, inner group.

Perhaps the most important point to see about the way Peter is portrayed in Mark is the fact that he is pictured in precisely the ambiguity that inheres in the picture of the disciples as a group. Mark will have nothing to do with a legendary tendency to exalt Peter. Peter is portrayed in all the grandeur and misery of the disciples of

Jesus as a group. Perhaps in the end these disciples are meant to show the kind of problems any follower of Jesus is likely to experience in the course of his attempts to follow his Master. If that is the case, then perhaps we can read from Peter's career Mark's comments on what it is like to be a follower of Jesus. It means to know supreme moments of faith as well as the slough of despair; it means "mountain top" experiences in the midst of which one's frailty and lack of perception intrude (cf. 9:2–8).

Even if the disciples, as Mark portrays them, may thus be intended to mirror the problems of any follower of Jesus, that does not exhaust their role. They do have an important place in Mark's narrative of the earthly career of Jesus, and that means in Mark's understanding of Jesus himself. Mark wants to make two further points, at least, in the way he portrays Jesus' intimate associates. The one has to do with the inevitability of suffering for one who follows Jesus, and the other has to do with the way Mark understands the way any person comes to understand Jesus. That is to say, it also deals with Mark's Christology. We must turn now to consider these two points.

Mark has put much of the material he had dealing with discipleship into chaps. 8–10 in his Gospel. We have already seen that this part of the Gospel cannot in any exclusive way be characterized as "Jesus teaching the disciples in private," since he has done that in earlier parts of the Gospel, and he continues to have contact with crowds in these three chapters. Nevertheless, a good portion of specific advice to the disciples is contained in these three chapters, and it is worth noting the structure into which they have been put.

First of all, it is just in these three chapters that we have the first sustained indications that Jesus' fate is to be suffering. The three predictions of his passion are contained in this section (8:31; 9:30–32; 10:33–34), and it is toward the end of it that we learn of Jesus' determination to go to Jerusalem (10:32). That in itself ought to be enough to alert us to the fact that a particular fate awaits those who follow a suffering leader. Mark makes that quite explicit, however.

He does that, in the second place, by the way he has ordered his material in this section. Immediately following each passion prediction, as we noted in an earlier chapter, there is a tradition that clearly shows the disciples' misunderstanding of the import of that prediction. Mark then places sayings of Jesus designed to correct the understanding of discipleship. It is worth looking at each in some detail. The sayings collected by Mark in the first grouping (8:34–38) make it clear, by means of paradoxical statements about losing and saving life, that concern for personal safety cannot be paramount for any of his followers. If the prospect of suffering and death would cause one to pull back from his devotion to Jesus (to be "ashamed" of him, v. 38), that person cannot become a disciple. Jesus must be of first and exclusive significance, or discipleship is out of the question (v. 34). It is worth noting that Mark has these words addressed not only to the twelve, but to the multitude as well. These words are directed to any who would follow Jesus, not just the inner circle.

The second segment concerning discipleship (9:35–37) is also given in paradoxical formulation (v. 35), and although specific emphasis on suffering is absent, its position within the repeated structure introduced by announcement of Jesus' impending death surely puts it within such a context. The third segment (10:42–45) continues the paradoxical formulation (to be great is to be servant; whoever would be first must be slave of all), which is then justified by a further statement about the fate of Jesus: he came to serve by giving his life (v. 45). Here is the clue to the paradoxical form in which these words on discipleship have all been cast: just as Jesus, the Lord of all, achieved lordship only through paradoxical paths of suffering and rejection, so those who follow him must carry that out in the same paradoxical way. Entry into the kingdom comes by the path of suffering and service; to reject Jesus' fate for oneself is to be rejected from that kingdom (cf. 8:38).

Clearly, it was important for Mark to emphasize the fact that there is no possibility of discipleship apart from suffering. Even when he came to repeat the tradition about the rewards of discipleship in this age (10:29–30), he included the little phrase "with persecutions" to make clear what the disciple can expect, and he concluded it with the typical paradoxical formulation about first and last (v. 30). The path to the glory of the kingdom of God leads through suffering, just as the path of Jesus to his lordship led through degradation and death on a cross. To follow Jesus means following him into suffering. Therefore, Mark began this section with the first explicit prediction of Jesus' suffering (8:31), and he ended it with a final statement by Jesus on the culmination of his mission: to give his life for others (10:45).

It is difficult to avoid the impression that this point on discipleship was a major concern for Mark as he shaped his narrative about Jesus. That may also explain the absence of any specific narratives about the risen Jesus. If, as we saw earlier, there was a tendency within the primitive church to want to come into direct contact with the risen Jesus, perhaps through a eucharist based on fellowship with Jesus the wonderworker who by rising from the dead proved his superior power, such a tendency would be very likely to downgrade, if not eliminate altogether, any emphasis on the suffering either of Jesus or of his followers. Paul corrected that tendency in Corinth with his emphasis on Jesus' cross (e.g., 1 Cor. 2:1–2), and by relating the eucharist to Jesus' suffering (1 Cor. 11:23). If Mark faced a similar understanding of Jesus, he may have chosen to meet and correct it by shaping his narrative in such a way that it climaxed with Jesus' suffering and death. There is no question that Mark knew that Jesus had risen from the dead (16:6). Yet he chose not to climax his narrative with those scenes. Whatever motive we may want to assign to Mark for omitting such resurrection narratives, or whatever fate we may want to believe about some other ending for this Gospel, in its present shape, the impact of Jesus' death on the cross continues in its effect on the reader even after he or she has read the concluding verses assuring us that Jesus rose from the dead. It may be that such an impact was part of Mark's intention.

It has also become clear in these last few pages that one cannot speak of Mark's view of discipleship without speaking of Mark's view of Jesus. His view of following Jesus is grounded in his Christology. Mark apparently was incapable of understanding Jesus in any other way than as the Jesus who suffered. That is the key to grasping the meaning of his career and of his fate. He is the one who gave his life as the ransom for many (10:45). The other side of that coin would seem to hold true equally well: any understanding of Jesus that failed to take his suffering and his death on the cross into account could only be false. The impending fate of Jesus is known from the early stages in Mark's narrative, and it is never far from the consciousness of Mark, or the sight of the reader. From the very outset of his public career, the opposition from Jewish religious leaders which was to prove fatal was present and active. The Gospel itself climaxes in the narratives of Jesus' passion and death, and the disproportionate amount of narrative space given to those final days would make clear the way Mark saw Jesus, if nothing else did. From beginning to end, the Jesus of Mark's narrative is the Jesus who will suffer, and unless that is understood, Jesus can only be misunderstood.

Again, the implication of a puzzling theme in Mark now becomes clear. If the disciples fail during Jesus' earthly career to understand him, it is for the simple reason that Jesus *cannot* be understood until his final fate is taken into account, and the disciples, in the course of the narrative, have not yet seen that final fate. The failure of the disciples to understand Jesus is thus grounded in Mark's Christology, not in the disciples' psychological makeup. But that failure has positive, not negative implications. The disciples fail to understand for the simple reason that no one can understand Jesus apart from knowledge, and acknowledgment, of his suffering. The persistent inability of the disciples to understand Jesus serves Mark's christological purpose: they have not seen the suffering and death of Jesus; therefore they cannot understand him. This may also explain the references to the "hardened hearts" of the disciples which precludes their understanding. God's plan clearly included the suffering of Jesus: the Son of man *must* suffer (8:31); he goes as it is *written* of him (14:21). There is thus no chance of perceiving that plan for Jesus until its climax has been accomplished, namely his death on the cross.

For Mark, therefore, the meaning of Jesus is not to be found in his words, important though they be, nor in his miracles, however much they may show about Jesus' lordship over the power of Satan. That is not where attention is to be concentrated, since those things will not lead one to understand the final meaning of Jesus. Those who are impressed by such words and such deeds, even encouraged by them to follow him, will fail to understand the true meaning of Jesus until they know he is the one who suffered. For Mark, the path of glory for Jesus led through the cross, and until that is understood, nothing is understood about Jesus. Small wonder the disciples failed to understand Jesus during his earthly career. Apart from his final destiny, they *could* not understand him. Neither can we, and that may well be a point Mark wants to make in his interpretation of the traditions about Jesus.

CHAPTER ELEVEN

THE PAROUSIA IN MARK

One of the major points, if not the major one, which the author of the Gospel of Mark wanted to make concerned, as we have seen, the great importance of the cross and resurrection of Jesus for understanding the meaning of his earthly career. Because those events came only at the end of his life, Jesus could not be understood by his followers until that climax had come. Conversely, because those events were the climax of Jesus' life, it is clear that for our author the path to glory for the disciples, as well as for Jesus, led through the valley of suffering. The cross therefore interprets both the life and the resurrection of Jesus, as it also interprets the way of following him.

On the other hand, the resurrection interprets the meaning of the cross, lifting it from an instrument of degrading death for one who challenged Jewish religious institutions and lost, to an event by which Jesus was shown to be vindicated by God despite the judgment passed on Jesus by state (Rome) and religion (Judaism). We have suggested that preoccupation in some segments of the early Christian community with the risen glory of Jesus may have led Mark to put the great emphasis he did on Jesus' suffering, thus correcting that preoccupation. To be blinded by the glory of the risen Christ was poor preparation for the persecutions that soon began to overtake his followers. For Mark there is no such glory without first the way of suffering. That insight may have led him to place the account of the transfiguration, which looks very much like an account of a resurrection appearance of Jesus, into the middle of his Gospel account, and to attach to it a discussion of the necessity of Jesus' suffering (9:2–13). Whether or not the transfiguration story is a "misplaced resurrection narrative" as some scholars have held, it cannot be disputed that the clearest story in Mark of the divine glory of Jesus is placed in the narrative in such a way that it is bracketed by references to suffering (8:34–9:1; 9:9–13). Therefore, it again makes that same point: the path to glory begins as the way of the cross.

Despite all that, Mark's Gospel remains incomplete in its present form. Surely there is more to this story than fearful women who have seen and heard things that defy understanding. They have been given an angelic commission: they are to tell Peter and the other disciples that Jesus has risen and will meet them in Galilee. We certainly expect at least a final account that they went there and found him, or that they heard the news and came to investigate the tomb, or at least that someone saw the risen Lord. As the narrative now stands, we are left up in the air. How does this story end?

It may well have been Mark's intention to give his readers the clear impression that in fact the events he has been narrating have not yet ended. If Mark understood the resurrection as the midpoint, as it were, in his story, with many significant events yet remaining to be played out, would there be a better literary way in which to convey that than to end his Gospel in such a manner that that impression is strongly left with its readers? Is there any indication that such was in fact Mark's view of the career of Jesus: that with the resurrection it had not ended, but was still underway?—that the final climactic events were yet to occur? The answer to such questions will be found by an examination of chap. 13, and, as we shall see, the answer is yes.

Chap. 13 has represented a perennial problem for students of Mark's Gospel. It interrupts the sequence of Mark's narrative. One could move from 12:44 to 14:1 without any difficulty whatsoever; the transition would be less abrupt, in fact, than from 13:37 to 14:1. The content of chap. 13 is also strange, and is of a different quality than the other traditions Mark has incorporated into his Gospel. It contains material of an apocalyptic flavor, and is much closer to the kind of writing we find in the Revelation of John than to the narratives Mark has assembled. Suggestions have been made that this material was added by Mark only after he had completed his narrative; or that Mark has taken an apocalyptic "pamphlet" that was circulating among the people for whom he was writing his Gospel, and because of its popularity, he was forced to include it, even though it contained material different from the traditions in which he was primarily interested; or that Mark worked these traditions into his narrative to correct an erroneous view of future events which was current in the Christian community to which he belonged and for which he was writing this Gospel. What such suggestions clearly show is that chap. 13 has represented a puzzle for modern interpreters of this Gospel.

The problematic nature of this material led an earlier generation of scholars to conclude that it represented the periphery of the Gospel author's interest, and that if he did include it, it was only because it was, in a sense, forced upon him. The remainder of his narrative showed where his real interest lay. In more recent studies, there has been a tendency to see in chap. 13 the key to the Gospel: Mark wrote his entire narrative to provide a framework for the reinterpretation of these apocalyptic traditions, and in this material we can catch sight of the events which prompted Mark to undertake the task of assembling his narrative. We will not be able to provide a definitive solution to this problem within the pages of this chapter, but we can take a careful look at this material, which may give us a perspective out of which to judge these various claims.

Chap. 13 divides itself into five sections set apart by the subject matter with which each deals. The first segment includes vv. 1–5a, and contains the introduction Mark has provided to this material. The fact that these verses alone relate chap. 13 to what preceded in chap. 12, and the presence of a characteristic Markan turn of phrase in v. 5a, attest to that. Vv. 5b–23 constitute the next segment, and deal with the theme that the end-time has not yet arrived; the present signs are preliminary. The segment begins and ends with references to false Christs who will lead many people astray (vv. 6, 22). The signs themselves can be divided into three types: wars, earthquakes, and famines (vv. 7–8); persecutions (vv. 9–13); and a "desolating sacrilege" which brings suffering in its train (vv. 14–23). Each of these paragraphs concludes with a comment on the material contained within it (vv. 8c; 13b; 23), providing further indication that this is the division intended by the author.

The next major segment includes vv. 24–27, and has as its point the assurance that after the preliminary signs enumerated in the preceding verses, the end will come in a form no one will be able to miss. There will be cosmic disturbances (vv. 24–25), the Son of man will come in all his power and glory (v. 26), and the elect will be gathered together from the whole world (v. 27).

The fourth major segment contains vv. 28–31, and centers on the affirmation that the end is coming soon. The preliminary signs indicate this (v. 29); indeed, the end will come within the present generation (v. 30; cf. 9:1).

The final major segment (vv. 32–36) contains the warning that no one is capable of calculating the exact time the Son of man is coming, since that is known only to God himself (v. 32). The proper attitude therefore is one of watchful, prayerful waiting, lest the imminent end catch one unaware (vv. 33–36). The entire chapter ends on that note of admonition: watch (v. 37).

As is by this time obvious, the chapter is not without its inner tensions. Coupled with the repeated warning not to assume that the signs delineated in the second major segment (vv. 5b–23) mean that the end is now at hand, there is the assurance that the end is indeed "near, at the very gates" when the reader sees "these things taking place" (v. 29). Coupled with the statement that the end will occur in "this generation" (v. 30) is the disclaimer that the time of the end is known to God alone (v. 32), a statement that must inevitably call into question any kind of statement about when it will take place. Furthermore, the "things" mentioned in v. 29 which show the end is at hand cannot refer to the immediately preceding events recited in vv. 24–27, since these latter verses indicate that when they happen the end is not imminent, it is present. In fact, if one were to remove vv. 24–27, and the repeated warnings that the end is not at hand which are scattered throughout vv. 6–23, one would have a statement that certain current events were the precursors of the end, and that therefore one should prepare oneself accordingly.

It is that kind of evidence that has led scholars to postulate that chap. 13 represents an apocalyptic pamphlet which was circulating, stating that events then underway signalled the beginning of the end. Mark has reworked that material by inserting warnings about false Christs, assurances that the signs are merely preliminary, an account of the kind of signs that will in fact presage the end, and a final disclaimer that any such calculation is likely to be wrong. In that way, he has transformed an apocalyptic attempt to reckon the time of the end on the basis of then-current events into an eschatological warning that the only appropriate attitude of the follower of Christ is watchful waiting. Such an explanation is certainly in accord with

Markan editorial techniques as we have encountered them in our examination of his Gospel (e.g., bracketing the material about signs with warnings about false Christs; insertions of editorial material that interpret the traditions with which he is working; furnishing the whole with an introduction which fits it into his narrative), and would certainly account for the inner tensions we find in the chapter. While absence of any objective evidence (e.g., existence of the original apocalyptic pamphlet) makes such a suggestion no more than a hypothesis, it does provide an attractive solution.

In addition to that kind of attempt to resolve the problems inherent in this material, there are some other observations we can make which may help to clarify our understanding of what Mark intended to do when he included it. We can see, for example, from the place in which Mark put this material, and the introduction with which he provided it, that he understood the problem involved in expectations of the coming Christ to be related in some way to the temple. The substance of the chapter is placed by Mark in the form of an answer by Jesus to the disciples' question about when the temple would be destroyed, a point Jesus had just mentioned. In addition, the chapter has been placed at the end of a long section in Mark in which Jesus has been pictured as active in the temple, beginning with its purging (11:11–25), and then continuing in a series of stories which Mark has placed in this setting (11:27–12:44). The climax of Jesus' sojourn in the temple is thus the announcement of its destruction in 13:2, just as the introduction of the section was Jesus' symbolic act of destroying its function (11:11–25). Clearly, then, the material about the problems attendant on expecting the end of the age and the quest for signs concerning it involve, in Mark's understanding, the temple in Jerusalem, and the events involving its destruction.

Whether Mark made use of an apocalyptic pamphlet that had connected its speculations about the imminent end with some mention of the destruction of the temple, or whether Mark himself was responsible for putting such speculations into this setting, is difficult to determine, especially since there is no mention of the temple after the introductory section Mark provided to the material (13:1–5a). The solution to that problem will do nothing to alter the fact, however, that in Mark's understanding, questions about when the end comes are tied to the temple. It would be attractive to suggest that it was the destruction of the temple under the Roman general Titus in AD 70 that prompted an outburst of speculation among Christians that now in fact the end was at hand, since God had ratified Jesus' judgment on the temple, and had destroyed any possibility of a Jewish religious alternative to faith in Jesus as Messiah. If that were the case, it would explain both the present setting of the apocalyptic material in Mark, and the warnings that despite events that parallel the expectations about the messianic woes (a Jewish belief that suffering would reach a peak of intensity just prior to the rescue by the coming of the Messiah) which are found in vv. 7–8, the end is nevertheless not yet imminent. This could also explain the reference to the "desolating sacrilege" set up in an inappropriate place, if that were to refer to the destruction of the temple by Titus, and its profanation as a result. A similar phrase is found in Dan. 9:27 in the context of a statement about the destruction of Jerusalem and its temple (9:26), probably during the reign of the Seleucid monarch Antiochus IV (ca. 167 BC; it precipitated the Macabbean revolt). Yet the advice to the reader in Mark 13:14 that special care must be taken to interpret that reference correctly indicates that Mark himself (or an early reader, if it is a gloss) was aware of the ambiguity of that reference. As a result, we are as little able to determine what that "desolating sacrilege" was as we are able to decipher what the author of the Revelation of John meant by the number 666 (or 616, as some other early manuscripts read; Rev. 13:18). It may have had no reference to the temple at all; we are unable to arrive at any kind of certainty.

A second observation to be made about this material in Mark is the fact that Mark associates it with the problem of premature claims that Christ has come again (vv. 6, 21–22). As we noted earlier, these references provide the framework within which the first segment of material is presented (vv. 6–23). Because such bracketing is a favorite Markan literary device, there is some reason to think Mark may be responsible for those references. In that case, the material serves as a vehicle for a warning against those premature claims, and represents a major concern for Mark in presenting these traditions. Apparently, because of the crisis referred to in vv. 7–20, claims were being made that Christ had in fact already come for the second and final time. There is, however, a subtle difference between the references in vv. 6 and 21–22. Clearly, vv. 21–22 refer to claims being made that Christ himself has returned (v. 21), and that individuals about whom such claims are raised are, because of the mighty acts they perform, gaining adherents (a further indication for Mark of the ambiguity inherent in miracles) for their false claims. The earlier reference (v. 6), however, could be interpreted to mean that men are claiming that Christ is present in them, and thus what they say, they say with the authority and power of the risen Christ who indwells them. While this would be further support for our earlier discussion about certain Christians who may have celebrated an "enthusiastic" eucharist, in which they claimed to share the wondrous power of Christ the "divine man," such a eucharist remains a matter of speculation, and the reference here in v. 6 could as well be interpreted in the sense of vv. 21–22. In fact, the repetition of the phrase about leading people astray (vv. 6, 22) tends to argue this latter case.

However one may want to decide that, it is clear that one problem, at least, which motivated Mark to include such material as this, lay in the fact that claims were being raised about a parousia that had already taken place (the same problem is faced in 2 Thess. 2:1–5), thus causing alarm among some Christians that they had somehow missed that key event. Mark not only assures them that such claims are premature and false, but also that when the Lord in fact returns, the attendant signs will be of such character that no one could possibly miss seeing them (vv. 24–26), and no follower of Jesus could possibly miss being included in it (v. 27).

A third observation to be made about this material consists in the fact that while Mark is at considerable pains to counter the idea that the parousia has already occurred, or is about to, he is also intent on assuring his readers that it will nonetheless come within the near future. With this he couples the strong urging that his readers be prepared for that event, and that discouragement at its temporary delay not tempt them to assume it has been delayed indefinitely. There is no other way that the material contained in vv. 28–37 can be understood. In fact, admonitions to watch or stay awake (some English translations reproduce these words with "take heed," "take care," "be on your guard") occur throughout chap. 13 (vv. 5, 9, 23, 33 twice, 35 twice, 37), and represent the only consistent theme within it. The conclusion of the whole chapter with its advice to the readers of the Gospel to be alert (v. 37), shows that this represented the main point Mark wanted to make. If there is a danger in Mark's eyes in premature expectation, there is an equal or greater danger in ceasing to look for the return of Christ altogether. If Mark wants to warn his readers by use of this material against premature claims that the end is imminent (vv. 7b, 8c, 10, 13b), he also wants to warn them that the end is nonetheless coming soon, and they had better be about the business of watching for it (vv. 30, 33, 35–37). Mark has thus taken an apocalyptic attempt to reckon the time of the end and turned it into an eschatological warning to be alert.

The logic of chap. 13 thus moves from warnings against premature claims about the parousia to admonitions to be alert, for it is coming in the near, if unreckonable, future. Clearly the parousia occupied an important place in Mark's understanding of the meaning of Jesus' career.

A final observation to be made centers on the references to the suffering which must precede the coming of Christ for the second time. If the material contained in vv. 9–13 draws on an apocalyptic pamphlet Mark may have used, it is clear that it has been edited by Mark to refer to Christian sufferings (if the pamphlet were Jewish), and to the universal mission of the followers of Christ (v. 10), a mission which he anticipated by placing several of the traditions he received into gentile areas (e.g., 7:24, 31). Christ's followers may not expect any other fate than that of their crucified Lord: they will be persecuted by Jews and gentiles (v. 9), and they will be hated for the simple fact that they are Christians (v. 13a). That, too, is a theme Mark had presented in the earlier part of his narrative (e.g., 8:34–35; 10:30). Disciples who undergo such harsh treatment experience the temptation to renounce the one because of whom they suffer. Therefore Mark points out that only those who endure to the end will be saved (13:13b). Once again, this point has been made earlier and explicitly in the interpretation of the parable of the sower (4:16–17). Those who would follow the risen Christ must, like him, endure such suffering to the end (cf. 14:34–36), if they would, like him, share in the glory of the resurrection.

Mark has therefore joined in this passage the themes of problems faced by contemporary Christians (false claims; national catastrophes; sufferings) with the assurance that the parousia which will deliver them from such tribulations is coming soon. That suffering should appear in this context of warning to contemporary readers of Mark's Gospel ought not surprise us; we have been amply prepared for that theme. That the parousia should receive such emphasis may seem a bit more strange, since we have made little of that theme up to now. Yet scholars are recognizing that it is in fact a key issue for Mark. Several have suggested (notably Marxsen and Perrin) that it is so important for Mark that he substituted it for the resurrection. The language by which Mark refers to seeing the risen Lord in 16:7 (the word for "see") is the same as that used by Jesus when he tells the high priest he will "see" the Son of man at his glorious return, thus showing the context within which Mark placed those words of the angel at the empty tomb. Jesus, in this view, thus directs his followers to return to Galilee for the final events, as Galilee was the scene for the original announcement of the coming kingdom of God (1:14–15). Christ will appear again where he preached and acted, this time to consummate the age and inaugurate visibly God's rule on earth.

One need not accept that view, however, to maintain the importance of the parousia for Mark. The word for "see" is the future tense of the same word Paul used in 1 Cor. 15:3–8 to describe the appearances of the risen Lord; since the disciples and Peter do not now see the risen Jesus, how else could Mark have described that act in the future except by using the future tense of the verb? Nevertheless, it would seem that the parousia is the key to understanding the ending of Mark's Gospel, even though 16:7 does refer to the resurrection. The key is provided by 16:8, and the indecisive way in which the Gospel ends. The resurrection is announced, and the reaction is one of ambiguity. The women "feared." The key to understanding who Jesus is has now been provided, as Mark has indicated all through his narrative it would be: with the resurrection, following the suffering, it will be possible to understand who Jesus really is. The resurrection has now occurred, Jesus can now be understood truly for what he is (the fact that Mark could write and that the gospel could be preached demonstrate that fact), and yet fear—and mystery—remain.

The risen Jesus is still the same Jesus as he was in Nazareth: he remains obscured by the events in which he participates. He taught and worked his acts of power in Galilee, and he yet remained obscure in his real identity and true meaning. He has risen, and yet he remains obscured by the events that continue to occur in the world: war, famine, persecution, false claims (as outlined in chap. 13). Only with his return in visible glory will that mystery finally be eliminated, will that obscurity finally vanish. Then even his enemies will have to recognize him for what he is (14:62); then the cosmos itself will announce his coming in signs no one can miss (13:24–25); then those who have remained faithful will experience the deliverance for which they have yearned (4:20; 13:13b). Yet until that time, mystery remains drawn over Jesus, now risen. The Jesus who drew rejection because of the ambiguity of his first appearance on earth continues in that same ambiguous way now as risen and powerful Lord. Only the final events will, once and for all, remove such ambiguity.

Therefore, the word for the readers of Mark's Gospel is: watch (13:37). Ambiguity remains: the women's reaction to the news that Christ had risen from the dead was—fear. Suffering remains: before Christ returns in his risen power, Christians will undergo unparalleled suffering in the course of the lives they lead as followers of their crucified and risen Lord. The possibility of rejecting Jesus remains: the world continues to throw barriers in the path to faithful discipleship in the form of "delight in riches, and the desire for other things" (4:19). Only at the end does the abundant crop appear. Only at the end does the grain ripen for harvest. Only at the end does the mustard seed produce the tree. The word remains, therefore: watch!

Mark has thus had much more in mind than just telling the story of Jesus of Nazareth. He has written an account aimed in the most direct way at his readers. Thus his narrative was shaped far more by what he thought was the contemporary significance of the traditions about Jesus than by any desire to reproduce the chronology of those events. His narrative was shaped far more by his desire to warn and encourage his readers than by any desire to solve questions of antiquarian curiosity about the career of this Jesus from Nazareth. Mark wrote to show the meaning those events have for the way life is to be lived now. The readers of this Gospel, then as now, live between the announcement that with Jesus God's kingdom dawns (1:14–15), and the promise of its final coming with his return in power and glory (14:62). It was also to tell what the traditions of Jesus of Nazareth meant, and mean, in that context that Mark set about the task of interpreting the Jesus traditions by creating out of them the tradition of the gospel of Jesus Christ.

CHAPTER TWELVE

SOME LITERARY PROBLEMS

With the completion of our examination of some of the major themes and theological issues contained in the Gospel of Mark, we are now in a somewhat better position to raise questions about the Gospel as a piece of literature: who wrote it, when, and where? Since the Gospel of Mark itself contains no statements about its literary origin, we must piece together such evidence as we can find, both in the Gospel and outside it, in our attempt to guess the answers. We will have to examine each piece of evidence to determine its reliability before we can use it in our solution. The problem we are faced with is very much like that of attempting to assemble a jigsaw puzzle without any certainty that all the pieces are there, or that the pieces we have before us come from the same puzzle. In such circumstances, certainty is difficult.

Some years after the Gospels were written, it became very important for the primitive church to know who wrote them, especially since a number of other gospels were also being produced, and one way to determine which ones were reliable was to know who wrote them. A reliable author would mean a reliable book. If the author were an apostle, it would help that much more in assuring that its contents were valid and useful for teaching within the church and for defending the church against claims about Christ being put forward in some other writings which the emerging catholic church later denounced as heretical.

Who wrote the Gospel of "Mark"? Perhaps the most important point to note with respect to that question is the fact that the author nowhere identifies himself (or herself; women played a prominent role in the primitive church, and especially in the Gospel we are investigating, e.g., 15:40–41, 47; 16:1–8, so there is no certainty about the gender of the author). Obviously, whoever wrote the Gospel felt that knowledge of the author's identity was of no importance in understanding the Gospel itself. The first readers may well have known who it was, but the fact that no attempt was made in this or any other of our canonical Gospels by the author to guarantee the readers would know who wrote it indicates the author attached no real significance to such information. The fact that our Gospel is composed largely of available traditions which the author ordered and connected may also have made identification seem pointless. The author was simply assembling material familiar to many readers, and was not composing in the sense that, say, Paul was when he wrote his epistles.

There are some hints in the Gospel itself that some scholars have taken as referring to the author (e.g., the seemingly pointless reference to the young man at the time of Jesus' arrest, 14:51–52), but even if these hints did identify the author, it would help us very little, since that is all the information we would have about him from the Gospel. The earliest evidence we have about the author of our Gospel comes from the church historian Eusebius, a bishop of Caesarea in the fourth century. Eusebius had the writings of an earlier man named Papias, who apparently lived sometime in the first half of the second century. Eusebius drew information from those writings in his *Ecclesiastical History*, and discussed it in book three, beginning with section 49. Papias is there identified as one who knew people who had known the apostles; he thus belonged to the "third generation" of Christians. Eusebius recounts what Papias said he learned from Aristion and John the Elder (who are otherwise unknown), namely that the author of our Gospel was a Mark who had been Peter's "interpreter" (it could also mean a kind of secretary–companion), and that he, Mark, wrote what he remembered of the things the Lord said and did (apparently from hearing Peter talk about those things), though he did not put them "in order." Papias then commented on that statement, affirming that Mark had not followed Jesus, but had followed Peter, and had attempted only to omit nothing of importance, not trying to "make an arrangement of them" (a historical account?). This tradition lies at the basis of our ascription of our Gospel to "Mark," since later traditions about the author clearly depend on this tradition from Papias. In fact, succeeding generations of Christians linked Mark ever more closely with Peter, having Mark write during Peter's lifetime, and finally at Peter's direction. That is simply an attempt to tie the Gospel ever more closely to an apostle so that apostolic authority could be claimed for it. In a similar way, tradition linked the author of the third Gospel, Luke, ever more closely with Paul. The basic insights of form criticism concerning the traditional nature of the Markan material constitute the chief argument against Papias' notion that the author of the second Gospel had been a companion of Peter.

On the assumption that there could have been but one Mark in the whole of the early church, every mention of anyone named Mark in the NT was assumed by some interpreters to be a statement about our author. Thus, the John Mark of Acts, who for a time accompanied Paul and Barnabas on their missionary travels, but later disagreed with Paul to the extent that Paul refused to have anything further to do with him (Acts 12:12; 13:13; 15:37–40), is identified with the Mark mentioned in Philemon 24 as Paul's "fellow worker." There is further mention of the name in Col. 4:10 (there identified as Barnabas' cousin), and in 2 Tim. 4:11 and 1 Peter 5:13. On the assumption that those names can only refer to one person, and with a generous dollop of imagination, the "author" of our Gospel has been created. That is, of course, a dangerous activity; Mark was perhaps the most common name in the Roman empire (e.g., Cicero and Brutus, as well as Marcus Aurelius and Mark Anthony, all bore that name), and the assumption that only one of them became a Christian is gratuitous. Many scholars seriously doubt that Paul wrote 2 Timothy, or that Peter could have written 1 Peter, and as a result those two letters really are more significant for the argument that there were several "Marks" than that we have in those places more information about the one Mark in the primitive church who wrote our Gospel.

On the other hand, no "Mark" emerges from the early church period prominent enough to warrant ascribing a Gospel to him. If apostolic authority was desired, ascribing it directly to Peter would have been much more effective. To that extent, ascribing it to Mark has a degree of historical probability for it. Our conclusion must therefore remain a tentative one: the Gospel may well have been written by someone named "Mark," about whom we know little else. We must resist the temptation of identifying the Mark who wrote our

Gospel with the Mark of Acts 12:12, whose mother, Mary, had an upper room in which early Christians gathered to pray, that upper room in turn being identified with the upper room of Acts 1:13. Then the false conclusion can be drawn that since from the beginning the disciples assembled in Mark's house, he had from eyewitnesses sure knowledge of the events of which he wrote. The final link is then the supposition that in that case, Mark wrote a reliable historical account of the actual course of events in Jesus' career. Not even Papias argued for that. Above all the Markan traditions which presupposed a period of oral transmission and the Markan geography and narrative frame speak against such conclusions.

Turning to the problem of the place where this Gospel was written we find that tradition has provided us with early speculation on this score as well. While Papias had nothing to say on this question, his identification of Mark as the "interpreter" of Peter, and Peter's traditional association with Rome, has led to the deduction that Mark, in Rome at the time of Peter's death, wrote the Gospel there. The cryptic mention of greetings from "Babylon," sent by the author of 1 Peter from "my son Mark" (1 Pet. 5:13) has been interpreted as further evidence that Mark was with Peter in Rome. Aside from the prevalance of the name "Mark" in the world of primitive Christianity, mentioned above, there is real doubt that Peter is in fact the author of this letter. But *if* Peter stands in some way behind this letter, and *if* the Mark mentioned there is the same "Mark" who wrote our Gospel, and *if* Babylon means Rome, as it does in Revelation 17–18, *then* this would be evidence that our Gospel could have been written in Rome, but it does not prove that it was written there.

Other evidence has been adduced to point to Rome as the place where our Gospel was written. For example, a number of "Latinisms" occur in the course of Mark's narrative (i.e., Greek words borrowed from Latin and spelled in Greek letters, such as centurion, denarius, legion, etc.), which, some have argued, would place the author in a place where the readers were familiar with Latin, i.e., Rome. That argument is specious for two reasons at least. First, such borrowing of words is common in any area where one culture assumes domination over another, especially military domination. The same thing happened with French words in Germany in the eighteenth and early nineteenth centuries, and with English words in

Germany since World War II. Anywhere Roman influence extended, therefore, such loan words would be found. Secondly, research has shown that those same words were taken over by the Jewish rabbis who transmitted the traditions assembled in the Talmud. Palestine would thus be as likely a conjecture of origin for Mark's Gospel as Rome on that basis, but in fact nothing at all can be deduced from such Latinisms.

Again, the repeated references to persecution in Mark's Gospel have led some scholars to assume that these are references to the persecution of Christians under Nero following the fire that devastated Rome. We know from ancient historians that the blame for that fire settled on the Christians, and they were subjected to some horrible tortures as a result. Yet the account of events in Mark 13 implies that the whole of the civilized world is in an uproar (13:7–8), but we have no indication that Nero's persecution of Christians extended much beyond the bounds of the city of Rome.

The fact that the author of Mark clearly associated those events related in chap. 13 to the destruction of the temple, as we saw, would argue for a point of origin affected directly by its fall in AD 70, i.e., Palestine. The description of 13:7–8 would fit the destruction brought about by the Jewish rebellion and its quelling by Roman legions in AD 66–70. The account of Josephus, a contemporary, mentions famines and earthquakes as well as national revolts, although such conditions may simply be a means of impressing on the reader the utter devastation those events brought with them. The problem with a Palestinian point of origin is twofold at least. In the first place, the author of the Gospel, or his traditions, assumed the readers would be unfamiliar with Aramaic, the common language of Palestine, and therefore all such phrases were translated into Greek (5:41; 7:34; 15:34). This would argue for an area other than Palestine. In the second place, the author is not at all clear on Palestinian geography (e.g., 7:31) or customs (6:17–28 has numerous errors in that regard), points that argue against a Palestinian origin. Some traditions of the second and third centuries put the place of origin as Egypt, a country where Clement of Alexandria said Mark carried on the first missionary activity, but that remains an isolated tradition.

As with the case of authorship, the point of origin remains obscure. Even the tradition that places Peter in Rome arose after the books in our NT were written. Acts knows nothing of Peter in Rome, nor does Paul refer to him when he writes his letter to the church in that city. Of course, none of that proves Peter did not get to Rome; it simply indicates how tenuous is the evidence that would put the writing of our Gospel in that city. Even the hints within the Gospel itself give us little help. The tumult described in chap. 13, even if it did refer to the war in Palestine in AD 66–70 would not necessarily locate the writing of the Gospel there. That war was known throughout the eastern Mediterranean world, and Titus thought his victory over the city of Jerusalem so important that he had a triumphal arch commemorating that victory erected in the heart of Rome.

In view of our uncertainty about the place where our Gospel was written, we must again be very cautious about using any such conclusion as a basis for interpreting the Gospel.

If the author and place of origin are obscure, we can hardly expect any greater certainty with regard to date. If, as seems almost certain, the authors of our Gospels of Matthew and Luke knew and used a form of Mark very like the one we have, then obviously our Gospel was written before either of those other two. Furthermore, if, as modern scholarship has rendered highly probable, the materials from which our Gospel was composed circulated for some years in Greek speaking areas as independent units, then we must allow enough time for this to have happened prior to the time the Gospel was written. Clearly identifiable references to any of our Gospels do not occur until well into the second century; references to sayings of Jesus similar to those in our Gospels may be as much due to the continuing oral traditions about Jesus as to the fact that a particular author had read one of our Gospels. Papias tells us he preferred the oral traditions to written accounts and in that he may not have been alone.

Tradition has again stepped into the breach and has assigned the Gospel to the years just after Peter's death in Rome, supposedly at the hands of Nero shortly after the latter's persecution of Christians got underway, i.e., sometime around AD 64. Scholars, noting the association of chap. 13 with the destruction of the temple, surmise a date around the time of the fall of Jerusalem, i.e., 68–70. From the way Matthew and Luke use some of the Markan material, and from other material they include which Mark does not have, some have surmised that while Mark was written before the fall of Jerusalem,

Matthew and Luke were written after it. For example, Luke omits Mark's reference to the abomination of desolation (Mark 13:14), and substitutes the words "when you see Jerusalem surrounded by armies (or army camps)." We know from Josephus' account of these events (*The Jewish War*) that the Romans laid siege to Jerusalem by establishing camps for the various besieging legions around the city. Luke 21:24, unique to that Gospel, describes Jerusalem as "trodden down by the Gentiles," which, because it is a more specific prophecy than in Mark, and because in AD 70 that is what happened, could also indicate Luke is writing after Jerusalem's fall. The reference to Jerusalem's fate in Luke 19:43 also reflects the way Jerusalem was captured. But it was standard Roman military procedure to build earth ramps against the walls of a besieged city until they were high enough for Roman troops to gain entry to the city over the walls, or to allow them to employ battering rams to level the walls. Therefore knowledge of how in fact Jerusalem was taken need not be presupposed by this verse in Luke. Matthew adds a reference to a city burned and its inhabitants murdered (22:7; Luke does not have this remark, although he and Matthew drew this story from a common source), which could reflect the fact that Jerusalem suffered such a fate, but again, it is not specific enough to allow us any certainty.

The description of conditions contained in Mark 13 could, of course, refer to the Jewish war of AD 66–70, but it could also refer to conditions in Palestine from, say, 37 BC, when Herod the Great waged war up and down Palestine seeking to impose his rule on the Jews, to AD 135 when as the result of yet another revolt Hadrian devastated the city of Jerusalem, as he thought once and for all. The absence of references to the fall of Jerusalem and the destruction of the temple in Mark proves nothing; there is no clear reference to those events in any NT writing, nor for that matter in the vast bulk of the Christian writing of the late first and early second centuries. Clearly, absence of such references is no indication at all that Mark was written prior to AD 70.

Anonymity seems to be what the author intended. Content to let the story of Jesus unfold and be judged on its own merits, our author makes no attempt to identify himself, the place, or the date of his writing. The traditions about Jesus can stand on their own, he seems to say, without any added prestige his name could bring.

SELECTED BIBLIOGRAPHY

A selection of recent studies in Mark

ACHTEMEIER, P. J. "Toward the Isolation of Pre-Markan Miracle Catenae" *JBL* 89 (1970), 265–91. "The Origin and Function of the Pre-Markan Miracle Catenae," *JBL* 91 (1972), 198-221.

An attempt by means of literary-critical study to isolate as a possible Markan source a collection of miracle stories which Mark incorporated in a non-eucharistic setting, contrary to their earlier use.

AMBROZIC, A. M. *The Hidden Kingdom.* The Catholic Biblical Quarterly Monograph Series, vol. 2. (Washington, D.C.: CBA, 1972).

The kingdom of Mark is future, yet already present; hidden, yet inevitably to be revealed at the end of time. A careful redaction-critical study of this major Markan theme.

BURKILL, T. A. *New Light on the Earliest Gospel.* (Ithaca: Cornell University Press, 1972).

A collection of essays, most of which appeared in scholarly periodicals; three of them concern Mark 7:24–31. Burkill has technical expertise, but keeps theological issues in view.

DONAHUE, J. R. *Are you the Christ?* SBL Dissertation Series, no. 10. (Missoula, Mont.: SBL, 1973).

A careful study of the trial narrative in Mark 14, which concludes that Mark was responsible for arranging independent traditions to achieve the present form of the account of Jesus' trial. Careful redaction-critical work.

KELBER, W. *The Kingdom in Mark.* (Philadelphia: Fortress Press, 1974).

Predicated on the assumption that Mark was written for the situation after the totally demoralizing fall of Jerusalem, Kelber shows how, in his view, Mark sought to interpret that event and its consequences.

MARXSEN, W. *Mark the Evangelist,* tr. J. Boyce, et al. (Nashville: Abingdon Press, 1969).

Written in Germany in the mid 50s, this book was the first serious attempt to apply redaction-critical insights to some problems of the Gospel of Mark. Examines what Mark intended with his treatments of John the Baptist, the geographical framework, the word "gospel," and chapter 13.

QUESNELL, Q. *The Mind of Mark.* Analecta Biblica, no. 38. (Rome: Pontifical Biblical Institute, 1969).

A careful methodological study, beginning with 6:52, that argues that Mark, in allusive ways, points in the first half of the Gospel to its final meaning explicated in the second half: Christ crucified and risen is present in the eucharistic worship of the church.

ROHDE, J. *Rediscovering the Teaching of the Evangelists,* tr. D. M. Barton. (Philadelphia: Westminster Press, 1971).

A survey of German studies in redaction criticism.

STEIN, R. "What is Redaktionsgeschichte?" *JBL* 88 (1969), 45-56.
The article deals with the rise, the definition, and the method of redaction criticism.

WEEDEN, T. J. *Mark, Traditions in Conflict.* (Philadelphia: Fortress Press, 1971).

The disciples are presented by Mark as representing a "divine man" Christology which Mark seeks to combat by his negative picture of Jesus' closest followers.

WREDE, WILLIAM. *The Messianic Secret,* tr. J. C. G. Grieg. (Cambridge: T. and T. Clark, 1971).

This classic study, done at the turn of the century, argued against the possibility of finding the kind of history in Mark necessary to write a life of Jesus. Basic insights are still valuable, though many details outmoded.

OLD TESTAMENT

1 Samuel
22:20 — 9

Psalms
2:7 — 35
8:4 — 45
21:12 — 89
35:11 — 89

Isaiah
6:9–10 — 69
42:1 — 35
53 — 89
56:7 — 24

Jeremiah
7:8–11 — 24

Daniel
7:13, 18 — 45
9:26 — 106
9:27 — 106

NEW TESTAMENT

Matthew
3:2 — 52
3:2–12 — 41
3:12 — 58
4:23 — 49
5:2 — 64
5:21 — 17
7:28–29 — 64
8:18 — 13
8:23 — 13
9:35 — 49
10:26 — 17
12:1–8 — 8
13:11 — 57
13:36–43 — 58
22:7 — 117
24:14 — 49
26:13 — 49

Mark
1:8 — 11
1:1, 2 — 49
1:4 — 52
1:7–8 — 41
1:9–11 — 35

1:10–11 — 44
1:14–15 — 49, 51, 52, 53, 109, 110
1:15 — 26, 41, 49, 53, 54, 55
1:16 — 95
1:21 — 61
1:21–22 — 62
1:21–27 — 63, 73
1:21–28 — 28, 29, 76, 80
1:25 — 80
1:27 — 64
1:27–28 — 94
1:28, 37 — 80
1:29 — 37
1:29–31 — 96
1:30–31 — 16, 75
1:32 — 85
1:32–34 — 30, 52
1:32, 35 — 84
1:34 — 79, 80
1:36 — 95
1:38 — 53
1:39 — 37, 80
1:40 — 74
1:40–45 — 53
1:44 — 79
1:45 — 80
2:1 — 12, 28, 48, 75, 94
2:1–10 — 75
2:1–12 — 46
2:1–3:6 — 86
2:2–4a — 75
2:4–5, 11 — 75
2:5, 10 — 76
2:7 — 93
2:7, 15, 18, 24 — 67
2:11 — 76, 80
2:12 — 76
2:13 — 28, 30, 61, 65, 80
2:13–17 — 12
2:15, 23 — 37
2:18–22 — 12
2:23–28 — 8, 16
2:25–26 — 16, 28
2:26 — 9
2:27–28 — 46
2:28 — 45
3:1 — 37
3:1–5 — 76
3:1–6, 22–30 — 70
3:2, 6, 22 — 67
3:5 — 80

3:6 — 48, 86, 87, 93
3:6, 7 — 38
3:7 — 94
3:7–9 — 80
3:7–12 — 30
3:9 — 65
3:11 — 36, 44
3:11–12 — 79, 80
3:16 — 95, 96
3:20–21 — 29
3:20–35 — 32, 33
3:21 — 73
3:21, 31 — 67
3:22 — 57, 63, 72
3:22–27 — 71
3:23 — 65
3:24–26 — 71
3:27 — 72
3:28–30 — 50, 57
3:31–35 — 29
4:1 — 37, 80, 94
4:1–2 — 30, 61, 65
4:1–12 — 33
4:1–34 — 67
4:2 — 65, 66, 67, 69
4:3, 9 — 66
4:10 — 37, 58, 66
4:10–12 — 69
4:10, 34 — 93
4:11 — 57, 59, 69
4:11, 12 — 66
4:12 — 68
4:13 — 66, 69, 93
4:13–20 — 69
4:14–20 — 54, 68, 69
4:15 — 70
4:16–17 — 70, 108
4:18–19 — 70
4:19 — 110
4:20 — 70, 110
4:21, 22 — 17
4:21–22 — 16, 66, 67
4:24–25 — 16, 66, 67
4:26–30 — 66
4:26, 27, 29 — 58
4:30–32 — 58
4:33 — 65
4:33, 34 — 66
4:35 — 13, 14, 66, 84, 85
4:35–41 — 77
4:35–8:26 — 77
4:38 — 62, 64

4:39 — 80
4:40 — 76
4:41 — 41, 80
5:1 — 13
5:1–20 — 77
5:7 — 36, 44
5:19–20 — 80
5:20 — 53
5:21 — 14, 80, 94
5:21–43 — 32, 33, 77
5:25–26 — 74
5:28 — 94
5:31 — 13
5:34 — 33, 80
5:35 — 62, 64
5:35–43 — 77
5:37 — 95
5:41 — 57, 115
5:42, 43b — 74
5:43 — 79
6:1–6 — 28
6:1–33 — 78
6:2 — 14, 37, 61, 64
6:2b–3a — 29
6:2, 6, 34 — 65
6:2, 47 — 84
6:3–6a — 29
6:4 — 45
6:4–6a — 63
6:7, 12, 13 — 62
6:7–31 — 32, 33
6:12 — 53
6:14–29 — 47
6:15 — 45
6:17–28 — 115
6:27–28 — 48
6:30 — 62, 80
6:30–34 — 30, 76
6:34 — 62, 94
6:35–44 — 30, 76, 77
6:43 — 30
6:44, 51 — 80
6:45 — 13
6:45–51 — 77
6:52 — 33, 57, 76, 93, 95
6:53 — 27
6:54–56 — 30
7:1–13 — 94
7:1–23 — 78
7:3–4 — 57
7:6, 9 — 93
7:14–23 — 33
7:17 — 37
7:18 — 57, 93
7:24 — 27, 80
7:24, 31 — 24, 27, 78, 108
7:25 — 94
7:25–26 — 74
7:26 — 27
7:30 — 80
7:31 — 13, 27, 115
7:32–35 — 75
7:32–37 — 53
7:34 — 57, 115
7:36 — 79, 80
7:36–37 — 75
7:37 — 74, 94
8:1 — 94
8:1–9 — 73, 77
8:1–10 — 30

8:10 — 80
8:11–12 — 73
8:17 — 57, 93, 95
8:17–18 — 73
8:19 — 30
8:19–21 — 29
8:20 — 30
8:21 — 33
8:22–26 — 34, 75
8:23–25a — 74
8:26, 27 — 39
8:27 — 25, 36, 96
8:27–30 — 36, 37
8:27–33 — 42
8:27–10:45 — 92
8:28 — 45
8:29 — 95
8:29–31 — 46
8:30 — 79, 80
8:31 — 34, 47, 48, 65, 70, 94, 95, 97, 98, 100
8:32 — 54, 93
8:32–33 — 34, 37, 55
8:33 — 43, 96
8:34–35 — 59, 108
8:34–38 — 34, 58, 98
8:34–9:1 — 102
8:35 — 49, 50
8:38 — 46, 48, 56
9:1 — 55, 104
9:2 — 85, 95
9:2–8 — 34, 44, 97
9:2–13 — 101
9:5 — 62
9:5–6 — 95, 96
9:9 — 46, 48, 79, 80
9:9–13 — 102
9:11–13 — 33
9:12 — 46, 47, 48, 95
9:14 — 37
9:14–27 — 77
9:14–29 — 33
9:17 — 62, 64
9:17–29 — 37
9:27 — 80
9:28 — 37, 93
9:28–29 — 77
9:30 — 80
9:30–31a — 37
9:30–32 — 34, 97
9:31 — 47, 48, 65, 70
9:32 — 33, 57, 93
9:33–34 — 34
9:35–37 — 34, 98
9:38 — 61, 62
9:38–41 — 34
9:41 — 42
9:43 — 55
9:47 — 56
9:52 — 80
10:1 — 37, 61, 65, 94
10:1–10 — 33
10:2 — 93
10:10 — 37, 93
10:17 — 61
10:17–25 — 70
10:17, 30 — 55
10:17–31 — 56
10:21 — 20
10:24 — 41

10:27 — 56
10:28 — 58, 94, 95
10:28–31 — 56
10:29 — 49
10:29–30 — 70, 98
10:30 — 108
10:32 — 97
10:33–34 — 34, 47, 97
10:34 — 48
10:35 — 61
10:35–41 — 34
10:38 — 93
10:42–45 — 34, 98
10:45 — 46, 47, 98
10:46–52 — 34
10:47–48 — 44
10:51 — 62, 64
10:52 — 80
11:1 — 84
11:1–14:72 — 93
11:9 — 94
11:11, 12 — 84
11:11–25 — 95, 105
11:12–14 — 73
11:12–25 — 23
11:13 — 95
11:17 — 37, 65
11:18 — 64, 87, 93
11:19, 20 — 84
11:20–21 — 73
11:21 — 62, 65, 95
11:27–33 — 86
11:27–12:44 — 105
12:1 — 87
12:1–11 — 86
12:1–44 — 56
12:9, 38 — 93
12:12 — 87, 93
12:13, 18 — 37
12:13–27 — 21
12:13–34 — 86
12:14, 19 — 61
12:28–34 — 19, 56
12:32 — 56, 61
12:33b — 20
12:34 — 56
12:35 — 65, 70
12:35–37 — 43, 86
12:35–38 — 37
12:37 — 94
12:38 — 65
12:41–44 — 86
13 — 25, 40, 55, 102, 103, 115, 116
13:1 — 61
13:1–5a — 103, 105
13:1–8 — 33
13:2 — 25, 89, 105
13:3 — 37, 95
13:5, 6 — 107
13:5b–23 — 103, 104
13:6–7, 8b, 10, 21–22 — 54
13:6, 22 — 103, 106
13:6–23 — 104, 106
13:7b — 108
13:7–8 — 103, 106
13:7–20 — 106
13:8c — 103, 108
13:9 — 107
13:9–13 — 103, 108

13:10 — 25, 49, 50, 53, 108
13:11 — 4
13:12–13b — 70
13:13b — 68, 70, 103, 108, 110
13:14 — 106, 117
13:14–23 — 103
13:21, 23 — 107
13:21–22 — 42
13:24–25 — 110
13:24–26 — 107
13:24–27 — 103, 104
13:26 — 46, 48, 68
13:27 — 68, 107
13:28–31 — 104
13:28–37 — 107
13:30 — 55
13:32 — 44
13:32–33 — 55
13:32–36 — 104
13:33, 35 — 107, 108
13:37 — 104, 107, 108, 110
14:1 — 84, 93
14:3 — 94
14:3–9 — 86
14:4 — 61
14:9 — 49, 50, 53
14:10–11 — 87
14:10, 17–18 — 88
14:12 — 84, 85
14:12–16 — 86
14:12, 17 — 87
14:17–20 — 87
14:21 — 46, 87, 95, 100
14:21–25 — 86
14:22–24 — 87
14:25 — 48, 55, 87
14:26 — 46, 88
14:27 — 87
14:28 — 38
14:29–31 — 59
14:30 — 87
14:31 — 54
14:32 — 88
14:33 — 95
14:34–36 — 108
14:35–40 — 88
14:37 — 95, 96
14:40 — 59
14:41 — 46
14:42 — 85
14:43–52 — 88
14:45 — 62
14:49 — 61
14:50 — 33, 88, 94
14:51–52 — 112
14:53–72 — 88

14:53b, 55, 65 — 89
14:58 — 25
14:61 — 42
14:61–62 — 46
14:62 — 48, 68, 89, 110
14:63–65 — 68, 88
14:66–72 — 59, 95
14:72 — 85, 96
15:1 — 85
15:1, 8, 18, 22 — 89
15:2, 9, 12, 18 — 43
15:11, 13–15 — 80
15:12–14 — 68
15:22, 34   57
15:26 — 43
15:29 — 25, 80, 88, 89
15:31 — 93
15:32 — 43
15:34 — 115
15:38 — 25, 36
15:39 — 44
15:40–41 — 35
15:40–42, 47 — 111
15:40–47 — 94
15:43 — 57
15:47 — 85
16:1 — 85, 94
16:1–8 — 111
16:6 — 99
16:6–7 — 91
16:7 — 38, 95, 109
16:8 — 91, 94, 109

Luke
3:1–17 — 42
4:31–32 — 64
4:31–5:11 — 94
4:36 — 64
5:29 — 12
5:33–39 — 12
6:1–5 — 8
8:10 — 57
8:22 — 13
10:25 — 19
11:33 — 17
12:2 — 17
12:8–9 — 56
19:43 — 117
21:24 — 117
24:13–27 — 3
24:44–45 — 3

John
2:13–22 — 12
2:19 — 89
2:22 — 3
14:25–26 — 3

16:12–14 — 3
21 — 91

Acts
1:13 — 114
6:14 — 89
10–15 — 93
12:12 — 113, 114
13:13 — 113
15 — 6
15:7 — 49
15:37–40 — 113
20:24 — 49

Romans
1:1 — 42
11:25–26a — 25

1 Corinthians
2:1–2 — 99
7:10 — 2
7:12, 25 — 2
9:14 — 2
11:17–34 — 78
11:23 — 99
11:23b — 78
11:23–24 — 2
11:23–25 — 86
11:23, 26 — 87
15:3–7 — 2
15:3–8 — 91, 109

Galatians
2 — 6, 93
2:20 — 4

Philippians
2:6–11 — 6

Colossians
4:10 — 113

2 Thessalonians
2:1–5 — 107

2 Timothy
4:11 — 113

Philemon
24 — 113

1 Peter
5:13 — 113, 114

Revelation
13:18 — 106
17–18 — 114